Herbert Puchta & Jeff Stranks
with Richard Carter & Peter Lewis-Jones

English in Mind

Second edition

Combo 3A
Student's Book

CAMBRIDGE UNIVERSITY PRESS
Cambridge, New York, Melbourne, Madrid, Cape Town,
Singapore, São Paulo, Delhi, Tokyo, Mexico City

Cambridge University Press
The Edinburgh Building, Cambridge CB2 8RU, UK

www.cambridge.org
Information on this title: www.cambridge.org/9780521279789

© Cambridge University Press 2011

This publication is in copyright. Subject to statutory exception
and to the provisions of relevant collective licensing agreements,
no reproduction of any part may take place without the written
permission of Cambridge University Press.

First published 2004
Second edition 2011

Printed in Lima, Peru, by Empresa Editora El Comercio S.A.

A catalogue record for this publication is available from the British Library

ISBN 978-0-521-27978-9 Combo 3A with DVD-ROM
ISBN 978-0-521-27981-9 Teacher's Resource Book 3A and 3B
ISBN 978-0-521-27980-2 Audio CDs 3A and 3B
ISBN 978-0-521-15586-1 DVD (PAL) 3
ISBN 978-0-521-17241-7 DVD (NTSC) 3
ISBN 978-0-521-17483-1 Classware DVD-ROM 3
ISBN 978-0-521-27982-6 Testmaker Audio CD/CD-ROM 3A and 3B

Cambridge University Press has no responsibility for the persistence or
accuracy of URLs for external or third-party internet websites referred to in
this publication, and does not guarantee that any content on such websites is,
or will remain, accurate or appropriate. Information regarding prices, travel
timetables and other factual information given in this work is correct at
the time of first printing but Cambridge University Press does not guarantee
the accuracy of such information thereafter.

Contents

Student's Book

Map of Student's Book		4
1	Welcome	6
2	Communication	14
3	A true friend	20
	Check your progress	27
4	A working life	28
5	Live forever!	34
	Check your progress	41
6	Reality TV	42
7	Survival	48
	Check your progress	55
8	Good and evil	56

Pronunciation	62
Vocabulary bank	63
Get it right!	66
Projects	69
Speaking exercises: Student B	71
Irregular verbs and phonetic symbols	72
Acknowledgements	73

Workbook

1	Welcome	76
2	Communication	80
3	A true friend	86
4	A working life	92
5	Live forever!	98
6	Reality TV	104
7	Survival	110
8	Good and evil	116

Grammar reference	122
Acknowledgements	126

1 Welcome	A Present simple vs. present continuous; question tags; ages; the environment		B Ways of talking about the future; gerund vs. infinitive; medicine and health; musical instruments

	Grammar	Vocabulary	Pronunciation
2 Communication	Past simple vs. present perfect simple	Body language *say* and *tell* Vocabulary bank: collocations with *talk* and *speak*	Sentence stress
3 A true friend	Past simple vs. past continuous review Time conjunctions: *as / then / as soon as* Past simple vs. past perfect simple	Friends and enemies Everyday English Vocabulary bank: friends	Linking sounds

CHECK YOUR PROGRESS

	Grammar	Vocabulary	Pronunciation
4 A working life	Present perfect simple vs. continuous review *had better / should / ought to*	Fields of work Jobs and work	/ɔː/ *short*
5 Live forever!	Future predictions First conditional review: *if* and *unless*	Time conjunctions: *if / unless / when / until / as soon as* Verbs with prepositions Vocabulary bank: verb + preposition combinations: *with/for/about*	Prepositions

CHECK YOUR PROGRESS

	Grammar	Vocabulary	Pronunciation
6 Reality TV	*make / let / be allowed to* Modal verbs of obligation, prohibition and permission	Television Extreme adjectives and modifiers Making new friends Vocabulary bank: extreme adjectives	/aʊ/ *allowed*
7 Survival	Present passive and past passive review Present perfect passive Future passive Causative *have* (*have something done*)	*make* and *do* Everyday English Vocabulary bank: expressions with *make*	Stress pattern in *have something done*

CHECK YOUR PROGRESS

	Grammar	Vocabulary	Pronunciation
8 Good and evil	Gerunds and infinitives	Noun suffixes Vocabulary bank: noun suffixes: *-ity/-ment/-ness/-ion/-ation*	Word stress

Pronunciation • Vocabulary bank • Get it right! • Projects • Speaking B • Irregular verbs and phonetics

C Present perfect simple with *for* and *since*; comparatives and superlatives; British English vs. American English; homes		**D** *used to*; *mustn't* vs. *don't have to*; information technology; noun suffixes	
Speaking & Functions	**Listening**	**Reading**	**Writing**
Talking about impressive things you have done Using body language Using expressions with *say* and *tell* Discussing animal communication	A text about methods of communication A discussion about body language	Article: Talking without speaking Culture in Mind: Talk to the animals	A composition about a person you have known for a long time
Predicting and retelling a story Discussing loyalty Last but not least: discussing meeting new people and making friends	A student retelling the story of Gelert	Story: Gelert: The faithful dog Quiz: Are you a loyal friend? Photostory: What friends are for	A story about two people meeting
Conversations with *How long ...?* Giving advice Job interview roleplay	A conversation about a job interview A job interview	Teenagers' blog comments about work Fiction in Mind: *The Book of Thoughts*	A letter of application
Talking about what makes people live longer Discussing stressful situations Last but not least: discussing future predictions	A radio show about longevity Song: *Live forever*	Article: Who wants to live forever?	A composition about the future
Talking about reality TV and fame Talking about rules at home Describing films, holidays, books and websites	A radio show about fame	Article: Ever fancied being on TV? Culture in Mind: Social networks	A report about a class survey
Talking about what will happen in the future Last but not least: discussing proposals to changes in your town	A presentation about changes in a town	Article: Bees dying for a phone call? Photostory: It's not really a choice	A formal letter to a newspaper
Finding out how well you know your partner Talking about computer games	An interview about someone's favourite computer game	Summaries of famous English novels Fiction in Mind: *The Water of Wanting*	A composition about the advantages and disadvantages of a chosen topic

1 Welcome A

* Grammar: present simple vs. present continuous; question tags
* Vocabulary: ages, the environment

1 Read and listen

a ▶ CD1 T2 Read and listen to Beth's diary entry. What did she and her parents disagree about?

September 12th

Dear Diary

Big argument with my parents tonight. I told them I want to go on a march next weekend to support environmental protection – and what did they say? Did they say: 'Good for you, Beth'? Did they say: 'Brilliant – we're really proud of you'? No chance. Mum said: 'A march? But marches are really dangerous, aren't they?' And Dad said: 'You're a bit young, aren't you?' I gave him my look. 'Dad,' I said, 'I'm 15. I'm not a child. I can look after myself.' Dad said: 'I know you're 15. That makes you a teenager, doesn't it? Not an adult!' And he and Mum started laughing. Why? Don't ask me. So I stood up and said: 'Look. You've heard about global warming, haven't you? Well, it's happening now. Now! Responsible adults try to do something about problems, right? And this is a problem! I'm a young adult now and I'm trying to do something. Ok? So I'll be on the march on Saturday.' Then I stood up and walked out of the room. Yay!

Now I'm sitting here in my bedroom. I can hear voices downstairs. Perhaps it's the TV, but actually I think it's my parents arguing. That's strange – they don't usually argue. Well, not with each other – only with me, of course!

b Answer the questions.

1. What is the march next weekend about?
2. What did Beth want her parents to say?
3. What reason does Beth give for wanting to go on the march?
4. Why does Beth think it is strange that her parents are arguing?

2 Present simple vs. present continuous

Complete the conversation. Use the correct form of the present simple or present continuous.

Isabelle: Hello?

Jamie: Hi Isabelle, it's me, Jamie.

Isabelle: Oh hi Jamie. Where ¹ _are_ (be) you?

Jamie: I'm in town.

Isabelle: And what ² _are you doing_ (do)?

Jamie: Shopping. I ³ _____ (look) for a new pair of trainers. But I can't find any good ones.

Isabelle: Try that shop in Princes Street. They ⁴ _____ (sell) really cool trainers there.

Jamie: Which shop? Oh, yes, I ⁵ _____ (know) it. It's called *Best Foot Forward*, isn't it?

Isabelle: That's right. My friend Alan sometimes ⁶ _____ (work) there at weekends.

Jamie: Really? Well, today's Saturday. Perhaps he ⁷ _____ (work) there today.

Isabelle: Hmm, well, I'm not sure. But go and see.

Jamie: I ⁸ _____ (go) there right now! Thanks for your help, Isabelle.

Isabelle: No problem, Jamie! Bye!

6 UNIT 1

3 Question tags

a Circle the correct words.

1. It's cold today, *has it / isn't it*?
2. He doesn't like me very much, *does he / isn't it*?
3. They're friendly, *don't they / aren't they*?
4. Your sister works very hard, *doesn't she / don't she*?
5. You went away last weekend, *didn't you / don't you*?
6. They won't come, *aren't they / will they*?
7. You can help me with this, *do you / can't you*?
8. She's got nice eyes, *hasn't she / isn't she*?
9. We should ask her, *don't we / shouldn't we*?

b Complete the conversation with the correct question tags.

Gary: Steve – you like football, ¹ *don't you* ?
Steve: Well, yes – sort of. But I'm not a good player. Why?
Gary: Well, we need another player for our team tomorrow. You'll play for us, ² _____ ?
Steve: Tomorrow? But tomorrow's Sunday, ³ _____ ?
Gary: No, it's Saturday.
Steve: Oh. Well, OK. I can play, I guess. But why don't you ask Billy Wright? He's a better player than me, ⁴ _____ ?
Gary: Billy Wright? He's only twelve. He's too young. I can't ask him, ⁵ _____ ?
Steve: So? If he's a good player, his age doesn't matter, ⁶ _____ ?
Gary: Well, I'll ask him. But we still need you anyway – we need two players for tomorrow!

c ▶ CD1 T3 Listen and check your answers.

4 Describing someone's age

Add the vowels to complete the words. Then number the boxes from 1 (the youngest) to 6 (the oldest).

- [4] t e e n a g e r
- [ ] _ d _ lt
- [ ] b _ by
- [ ] p _ ns _ _ n _ r
- [ ] ch _ ld
- [ ] t _ ddl _ r

5 The environment

a Read the text and complete the puzzle.

It's up to all of us to look after the environment. So what can we do?

👍 Use less paper. Paper comes from trees, and we need to protect the ² *forests* where trees grow.

👍 ⁴ _____ things like glass and plastic. When we use things more than once, we help to protect our environment.

👍 Turn off taps when you aren't using the water. Water is a very precious thing, and we shouldn't ⁶ _____ it.

👍 Don't ⁸ _____ ³ _____ on the streets! Always put your ⁷ _____ in a bin, or take it home and put it in the bin there!

👍 Try to travel less by car or plane. Cars and planes produce ⁵ _____ which pollute the ¹ _____ . And remember – that's the air that we breathe, so we should do our best to keep it ⁹ _____ !

Crossword (vertical word: POLLUTION)
- 2: FORESTS

b ▶ CD1 T4 Listen and check your answers.

1 Welcome B

* Grammar: ways of talking about the future; gerund vs. infinitive
* Vocabulary: medicine and health

1 Read and listen

a ▶ CD1 T5 Read and listen to the messages. Why is it important for Andy that Nadia plays on Saturday?

 Andy, I don't think I'll be able to play on Saturday night – sorry.   **Nadia**

 What??!! Why not, Nadia? We need you. It's an important night and we can't get another trumpet player before then. And no one in the band can learn to play the trumpet in three days!   **Andy**

 I'm in bed with a cold and a temperature. No way can I play the trumpet right now.   **Nadia**

 Well it's only Wednesday. Surely you'll be better on Saturday?   **Andy**

 Perhaps, but I can't practise at the moment, obviously. My throat hurts too much. So I've decided to stay in bed.   **Nadia**

 Well are you doing anything about your cold? Are you taking any medicine? Perhaps your doctor can give you an injection.   **Andy**

 Hey Andy, thanks for the understanding. I'm ill here! I don't enjoy having a temperature, you know. I can't stand lying here and doing nothing!   **Nadia**

 OK, sorry – but you have to play on Saturday. Some people from a recording company are coming. They're looking for new jazz bands like us. It's our big chance!   **Andy**

 What? Really?   **Nadia**

Yes, really. If they think we're good enough, they might offer us a record deal!   **Andy**

 OK, I promise to try. I'll do everything I can to get better. I hate being ill and I don't want to let you down. I'm going to get better! Let's chat again tomorrow.   **Nadia**

OK. Thanks a lot. Get well soon, OK? I mean it!   **Andy**

b Mark the sentences T (true) or F (false). Correct the false statements.

1. Nadia is the trumpet player in a band. **T**
2. There are two days to go before the band plays. ☐
3. Nadia's got a sore throat. ☐
4. Nadia thinks Andy is being very understanding. ☐
5. A record company wants new jazz bands. ☐

2 Ways of talking about the future

a Look at the pictures and circle the correct words.

1. *We'll have /* (*We're having*) a party next Saturday – do you want to come?

2. The sky's getting darker – I think *it's raining / it's going to rain*.

3. It's possible that in 50 years there *won't be / aren't going to be* any tigers in the world.

4 *I won't study / I'm not going to study* medicine – I want to be an actor now.

5 I've got an appointment with the doctor – *I'm seeing / I'll see* her at 10 o'clock tomorrow.

6 Thanks Annie. *I'll give / I'm giving* it back to you tomorrow – promise!

b Complete the sentences with the correct future form. Use the word at the end to help you. For arrangement use present continuous; for prediction use *will/won't*; for intention use *going to*.

1 I've got a date with Phil tonight – I *'m meeting* (meet) him at 8 o'clock. **arrangement**
2 I've missed my bus, so I .... (walk) home. **intention**
3 In 2099, it .... (be) impossible to tell the difference between people and robots. **prediction**
4 I think someone .... (break) the 100m running record at the next Olympics. **prediction**
5 My parents .... (visit) my uncle and aunt next weekend. **arrangement**
6 My friend Megan .... (study) languages at university when she leaves school. **intention**
7 My parents .... (not give) me a new computer for my birthday – no way! **prediction**
8 Sorry, I can't meet you this afternoon – I .... (play) squash with Joe. **arrangement**
9 OK, I've finished my homework – now I .... (watch) some TV. **intention**

3 Gerund vs. infinitive

Circle the correct words.

1 My sister hates *speaking* / *to speak* foreign languages.
2 My friend Tom's really kind. He enjoys *to help / helping* other people with their problems.
3 The homework was really difficult, so my mum offered *helping / to help* me.
4 I can't stand *washing / to wash* my hair!
5 We missed the train, so we decided *to wait / waiting* for the next one.
6 Mum's car is really dirty, so we've promised *washing / to wash* it for her tomorrow.
7 I'm not in a hurry, so I don't mind *to wait / waiting* for another fifteen minutes.
8 My holiday in the USA was great. I learned *to play / playing* American football!

4 Medicine and health

Complete the sentences with the words in the box. There are two words you will not use.

> epidemic pain hurt temperature patient ~~ambulance~~ surgeon cold sore injection

1 There's been a bad accident. Please send an *ambulance*, quickly!
2 Be careful, or you'll fall off your bike and .... yourself.
3 I feel awful – I've got a .... of 39 °!
4 Doctor, I've got a really bad .... in my shoulder.
5 The dentist gave me an .... , and I didn't feel anything after that.
6 Can I see Doctor Smith please? I'm a .... – my name is Gore.
7 I can't really speak right now – my throat's very .... so I don't want to talk.
8 My aunt's going to have an operation next week, but the .... says everything will be OK.

1 Welcome C

* Grammar: Present perfect with *for* and *since*; comparatives and superlatives
* Vocabulary: British English vs. American English, homes

1 Read and listen

a Read the interview with Pietro, an Italian student. Match the questions with the answers. Write A–E in the boxes.

A Do you miss your family and friends?
B Is there anything about England that surprises you?
C How long have you been here, Pietro?
D How long do you think you'll stay?
E Have you had problems with the language?

b ▶ CD1 T6 Listen and check your answers.

What do you think about England?

1 ___ Since the beginning of the summer. I've just finished an English course to prepare for my Proficiency exam. My speaking's good, but I have to work hard on my reading and writing!

2 ___ Yes, of course I do. But some people have come to visit me. Actually, my mother is visiting me right now. She's been here for two weeks. I think she's making sure that I'm eating properly!

3 ___ Well, yes, one thing. It's amazing how important houses and homes are to British people! My host family lives in a semi-detached house with a garden at the back, and they spend all their time and money on the house or the garden. At the weekend, everyone near here cuts the grass in their garden. It's incredible!

4 ___ Yes – quite a few. The English I learned in Italy was mostly American English – so when a guy here asked me one day if I wanted a lift home, I was a bit confused! I mean, I know that 'lift' in British English is what the Americans call an elevator – but I didn't know that 'a lift' can also mean 'a ride'. And the accent here! It's cool – but it's the strangest thing I've ever heard, too!

5 ___ I don't know. I haven't really thought about it. Six months? A year? Maybe if I like it, I'll never leave! Well, no, that's another joke – I mean, one day I'll go home to Italy, I'm sure of that. But only after I've passed the Proficiency exam!

2 Present perfect simple with *for* and *since*

a For each sentence below, two endings are possible and one is not. Cross out the ending that is not possible.

1	My life has changed since …	~~more than a month.~~	I went to Spain.	I met her.
2	I haven't seen him for …	two weeks.	a long time.	I was born.
3	I've had this photo for …	the first time I saw you.	the last six weeks.	years.
4	We haven't spoken since …	as long as I can remember.	Frankie's party.	last Friday.
5	We've lived here for …	over fifteen years.	most of my life.	1998.
6	I've loved sport since …	the first time I played football.	a long time.	I was a child.

b Write questions with *How long …?*

1 you / know your best friend?
2 you / like your favourite band?
3 you / live in your house?

c Ask a partner your questions from Exercise 2b.

10 UNIT 1

3 Comparatives and superlatives

Complete the text. Write the correct form of the adjective in brackets, and add any extra words needed.

Paris or London? A lot of British people love Paris, and a lot of French people love London. We asked people who know both cities to give us their opinion.

Jean-Pierre:
I love both places, but I think Paris is a lot ¹ *more beautiful* (beautiful) than London. And of course the weather is a lot ² _____ (good) in Paris too!

Amy:
For me, there's no question – London is the ³ _____ (great) city in the world. I mean, Paris is lovely, the people there are great – but Paris isn't ⁴ _____ (exciting) as London.

Françoise:
I prefer Paris – sorry, but it's true! It's the ⁵ _____ (beautiful) city in the world, and they have the ⁶ _____ (good) food in the world there, too. I don't think London is ⁷ _____ (interesting) as Paris – I mean, for things like shops and museums and history, Paris wins every time.

Alan:
Wow, that's a hard question. I love both places. I don't think Paris is ⁸ _____ (attractive) as London but London is just ⁹ _____ (interesting) as Paris. And the two cities are ¹⁰ _____ (expensive) as each other, so it's hard to choose. But in the end … yes, Paris, I guess.

4 British vs. American English

Add the vowels to complete the American English words. Then match them with the British English words.

British English	American English
1 biscuits	a) __ l __ v __ t __ r
2 flat	b) s __ d __ w __ lk
3 football	c) c o o k i e s
4 lift	d) c __ ndy
5 lorry	e) g __ rb __ g __
6 pavement	f) p __ nts
7 rubbish	g) s __ bw __ y
8 sweets	h) s __ cc __ r
9 trousers	i) __ p __ rtm __ nt
10 underground	j) tr __ ck

5 Homes

a Look at the picture and complete the text.

I live in a block of ¹ *flats* . Our place is on the first ² _____ – I'm happy about that, because if the lift isn't working, I can walk up the ³ _____ . Our place is all right, but I really like my grandparents' place – it's a ⁴ _____ house, with lots of space around it, and they've got a big ⁵ _____ , big enough for two cars. There's a ⁶ _____ at the back, with grass and a tree and flowers, and a wooden ⁷ _____ all the way round it. It's really nice – but unfortunately, my grandparents have got a ⁸ _____ that they use when they go on holiday, and they keep it in the garden – it looks really ugly!

b ▶ CD1 T7 Listen and check your answers.

UNIT 1

1 Welcome D

* Grammar: *used to*; *mustn't* vs. *don't have to*
* Vocabulary: information technology, noun suffixes

1 Read and listen

a ▶ CD1 T8 Read and listen to the article. What is 'it' in the headline?

It's legal – but is it right?

When people wanted to find their way to a place in the past, they used to have to buy a map. They don't have to do that any more. Now they can either buy a GPS, or go online and find maps for just about anywhere.

Is this an improvement? Perhaps, but some people think some of the online companies are going too far, because they have been sending out cars with photographic equipment on their roofs, to photograph every street and house in the country.

One of these cars arrived on a Wednesday morning in the quiet English village of Broughton. The camera was on a metre-high pole on top of the car and could see over walls and into people's gardens. Some of the villagers came and stood around the car, and asked the driver and photographer to go away. Journalists quickly arrived on the scene, and soon the event was news all over the country.

Of course, the online company in question claims that it is simply collecting information that people on the internet want. But Broughton residents feel differently.

'We used to have privacy in this country – now companies just come and take photographs of our homes without even asking,' said one resident. 'It's not right. We mustn't let this happen. We mustn't lose our right to live privately.'

There is, of course, no law to prevent people from taking photographs of houses, so the residents cannot go to court. But many people are asking the question: 'OK, it's legal, but is it right?' This is a question that won't go away very …

b Read the article again. Answer the questions.

1. What did people do in the past to find their way to places?
2. What do people do now to find their way to places?
3. Why do some people think online companies are going 'too far'?
4. What did the villagers of Broughton want the driver and photographer to do?
5. Who else appeared in the village?
6. Why was one resident of Broughton not happy about the photographs?
7. Why can't the people who live in the village go to court?

2 used to

Complete the sentences. Use the present simple for one verb, and the correct form of *used to* with the other verb.

> be (x3)   go (x3)   like (x2)   read   sell
> smoke   think   work (x2)   want   ~~walk~~

1. I *used to walk* to school when I was a kid, but now I ____go____ by bike.
2. My father _____ in a bank, but now he _____ for a car hire company.
3. That shop _____ terrible, but two years ago it _____ really nice things.
4. We _____ to Spain for our holidays now, but we _____ going to Italy.
5. I _____ a good singer any more, but I _____ the best singer in my school.
6. My mum _____ that magazine every week, but now she _____ it's boring.
7. I _____ living in a flat, but now I really _____ to live in a house.
8. People _____ in restaurants in Britain, but now they _____ outside to smoke.

12 UNIT 1

3 mustn't vs. don't have to

Complete the sentences with the phrases in the box.

> We mustn't be   You mustn't play   ~~You mustn't eat~~
> You don't have to eat   We don't have to be   You don't have to play

1 This is a library. _You mustn't eat_ in here.
2 _____ it if you don't like it.
3 _____ with matches.

4 _____ if you don't want to.
5 _____ late!
6 _____ nervous – it's only a test.

4 Information technology

Complete the nouns and verbs with the words from the box.

> ~~board~~   word   drive
> stick   lead   pad   slot
> on   load   work

1 a key_board_
2 a CD _____
3 a memory _____
4 to down_____
5 to log _____
6 a pass_____
7 a power _____
8 a net_____
9 a touch_____
10 a USB _____

5 Noun suffixes

Write the correct form of the word in brackets.

1 Did you get an _invitation_ to Sarah's party next week? (invite)
2 The best thing about swimming is that you don't need much _____ . (equip)
3 She works for the local newspaper – she's a _____ . (journal)
4 Sorry, there are no tickets left – but try again tomorrow, we might get a _____ . (cancel)
5 You can only eat in that restaurant if you make a _____ about two weeks before. (reserve)
6 He's still quite ill, but the doctors think there'll be some _____ soon. (improve)
7 My brother works as a _____ in a hotel in London. (reception)
8 He studied hotel _____ at university. (manage)
9 He hopes that one day he'll be the _____ of a hotel somewhere. (manage)
10 I don't watch football on TV any more – I just don't think it's very good _____ (entertain)

2 Communication

* Past simple vs. present perfect simple
* Vocabulary: body language, *say* and *tell*

1 Speak and Listen

a Work with a partner. Think about the three methods of communication you use the most. Discuss the advantages and disadvantages of each one.

b ▶ CD1 T9 Listen to someone talking about methods of communication. Which of the following are NOT mentioned?

> body language   braille
> phone calls   sign language
> telepathy   Morse code

c Which of the methods of communication in Exercise 1b do you think is most effective? Discuss your ideas with your partner.

2 Read and listen

a Discuss these questions.
1 Do you know anyone who has a twin brother or sister?
2 Do you think twins have any special ways of communicating?

b Read the article quickly and answer these questions.
1 What methods of communication between twins are mentioned?
2 What happens to some twins when their brother or sister has a bad experience?

Talking without speaking

1 Parents of twins often say their children are a little unusual or a bit special. But according to 16-year-old twin Gerald Scott, there are ways in which some sets of twins are quite amazing.

'My twin, Owen, and I have had a very special bond since we were 5 born. When we were very small, we had our own language. Our mum says we used to talk to each other using our own special language. We knew what we were saying but nobody else understood. Even our mother didn't understand us! As we've got older, we've started using telepathy to communicate. Sometimes we don't need to speak at all; 10 we just use our minds. We can somehow send messages to each other even when we aren't in the same place. I know it sounds weird, but I've always known if Owen was in trouble. Once he had a bad fall in rugby – he broke his leg and when it happened, I got this terrible pain in my leg.'

15 Although it sounds strange, telepathy between twins isn't so unusual. There has been a lot of research that has proved that some twins have this ability. One experiment involved eight-year-old Richard Powles and his twin, Damien. First, they were put in separate, sound-proof rooms, and Damien was wired up to a machine that measured his responses. 20 Richard was then asked to put his arm into freezing cold water. At the exact moment he put his arm into the water, Damien's responses went wild. And it was the same whenever anything scary or surprising happened to Richard – his brother in the other room reacted too.

There have been cases between celebrity twins too. Actor Ashley 25 Olsen tells us that, even when they are far apart, she knows when her twin sister, Mary-Kate, is going through a difficult time or when she isn't happy. So, maybe it's true – maybe some twins don't need words at all to speak to each other.

c ▶ CD1 T10 Read the article again and listen. Mark the statements *T* (true) or *F* (false). Correct the false statements.

1 Only their mother could understand Gerald and Owen's special language when they were small. ☐
2 Gerald and Owen can communicate even if they are in different places. ☐
3 According to the text, it is rare to hear of telepathy between twins. ☐
4 Damien wasn't able to see Richard or hear anything he said during the experiment. ☐
5 Ashley Olsen has experienced telepathic communication with her twin. ☐

Discussion box

1. Lots of people think telepathy is not possible. What's your view?
2. What would be good (or not so good) about being telepathic?
3. What new ways might we use to communicate with each other in the future?

3 Grammar

✱ Past simple vs. present perfect simple

a Look at the examples from the text. Which of the sentences are in the past simple, and which are in the present perfect simple?

*Owen and I **have had** a special bond between us since we were born.*

*Once he **had** a bad fall in rugby.*

*One experiment **involved** eight-year-old Richard Powles and his twin, Damien.*

*There **have been** cases between celebrity twins too.*

b Find other examples in the text. Underline examples in the past simple. Circle examples in the present perfect simple.

c Complete the rule. Write *past simple* or *present perfect simple*.

> **RULE:** We use the .... to talk about events in the past which are separate from now (the moment of speaking).
>
> We use the .... to connect the past and now (the moment of speaking).

*He **broke his leg** and when it happened, I got this terrible pain in my leg.*

*Owen and I **have had** a special bond between us since we were born.*

✱ Time expressions

d Complete the rule. Write *past simple* or *present perfect simple*.

> **RULE:** We use the .... with expressions such as *last week, a year ago, in June, yesterday* (referring to time completely in the past).
>
> We often use the .... with *for* and *since* (the period of time is from the past to now).
>
> We usually use the .... with *just, already* and *yet* (words that have a link with now).
>
> We often use the .... with *ever* and *never* (referring to any time up to now).

e Complete the text. Use the correct form of the past simple or the present perfect simple.

Petra Dawes ¹ ....*left*.... (leave) school six months ago. But she ² .... (not go) straight on to university after the holidays like a lot of her schoolmates. In September she ³ .... (do) something she had wanted to do for some time. She ⁴ .... (take) a gap year. Since then, she ⁵ .... (travel) to three different countries and ⁶ .... (spend) between two and four weeks in each one. She ⁷ .... (not learn) three new languages though, because all the countries are French-speaking! But she ⁸ .... (start) to learn some Italian, because Italy is her next stop – and she can't wait! 'I ⁹ .... always .... (want) to see Italy. It's a country I ¹⁰ .... never .... (visit), so I'm incredibly excited about it!'

4 Speak

Imagine you've just done something really impressive. Tell a partner. Your partner quickly invents something that he or she did before that was even more impressive.

Think about pop stars, famous actors, extreme sports, exciting travel destinations, etc.

A: *I've just met Jay-Z.*

B: *Oh, really? He invited me to a gig last year, but I couldn't go.*

5 Listening and vocabulary
✱ Body language

a ▶ CD1 T11 Match the words with the pictures. Then listen, check and repeat.

1. make eye contact
2. fold your arms
3. lean forward
4. sit back
5. avoid eye contact
6. gesture
7. raise your eyebrows
8. look nervous
9. give someone a warm smile
10. nod your head

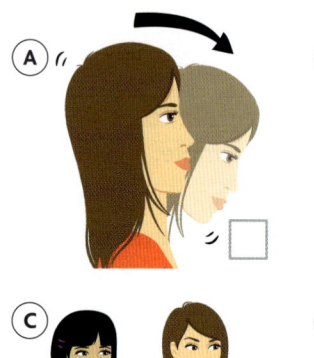

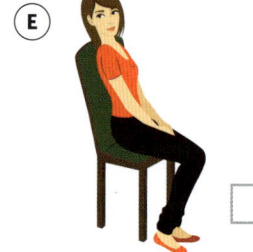

c ▶ CD1 T12 Listen to Oliver and Francesca doing a quiz about body language. Circle the correct answer a, b or c.

1. Everyone uses body language:
   a. intentionally.
   b. without knowing it.
   c. when they want to read someone's mind.
2. Francesca thinks that when people fold their arms, they are feeling:
   a. happy.
   b. bored.
   c. defensive.
3. Oliver says that arm folding can also be a sign of:
   a. feeling cold.
   b. being annoyed.
   c. wanting to protect somebody.
4. Oliver is surprised:
   a. that 90% of communication is done through body language.
   b. that body language isn't more reliable.
   c. that speaking is as important as body language.
5. Mirroring is a sign that:
   a. you are boring people.
   b. someone likes you.
   c. someone thinks they are similar to you.
6. The eyebrow flash is:
   a. something that people choose to do.
   b. something you can only do when smiling.
   c. done all over the world.

6 Speak

a Work with a partner.

Student A: Choose one of the topics in the box. Talk to your partner about it for one minute.

Student B: Use body language to show that you are a good listener. Swap roles.

> something you bought recently
> an interesting film   your favourite place
> your plans for next weekend

b Now do the same thing with the other two topics, but this time be a bad listener.

c What difference did your body language make to communication?

b Work with a partner. Tick (✔) the things in Exercise 5a that help communication and cross (✘) the ones that do not help communication.

7 Vocabulary

* say and tell

a Complete the sentences from the conversation in Exercise 5c. Use the correct form of *say* or *tell*.

1 Someone's body language _tells_ you how they are feeling.
2 When someone crosses their arms, it _____ us they want to protect themselves.
3 About 90 percent of what we _____ isn't spoken. We communicate a lot through our body language.
4 Can you _____ me what it means?
5 A: What automatic gesture do people do when they meet someone they like?
   B: Well, I'd _____ they smile.
6 The quiz _____ we do the 'eyebrow flash' when we see someone we like.

b Complete the sentences. Use the correct form of *say* and the words in the box.

> it out loud   thank you   sorry   it again   ~~goodbye~~

1 Don't leave until you have _said goodbye_ .
2 When someone has done something for you, you should _____ .
3 When you have hurt someone, you can make it better by _____ .
4 When you say what you're thinking so that people can hear, you _____ .
5 If someone didn't hear you, it helps to _____ .

c Complete the sentences. Use the correct form of *tell* and the words in the box.

> a lie   ~~a joke~~   a secret   the truth   off   the difference

1 My friend _told_ me _a joke_ yesterday – it was very funny, but now I can't remember it!
2 One day when I was little, I _____ my parents _____ and they were very angry.
3 Can you _____ between an American accent and a British accent?
4 My teacher was so angry with me. She really _____ me _____ .
5 He says he's won medals for tennis, but I don't think he's _____ .
6 I'm going to _____ you _____ . Do you promise not to tell anyone else?

Vocabulary bank Turn to page 63.   **Get it right!** Turn to page 66.

8 Speak

Work with a partner.
Student A: Complete the questions with *say* or *tell*. Then ask your partner the questions.
Student B: Turn to page 71.

1 Did your parents always make you _____ 'please' and 'thank you' when you were younger?
2 How many times have you _____ 'I love you'?
3 Can you _____ me a funny joke?
4 Can you _____ what you did on your last three birthdays?
5 When was the last time you _____ a lie, and what was it?

9 Pronunciation

* Sentence stress

▶ CD1 T13   Turn to page 62.

UNIT 2   17

Culture in mind

10 Read and listen

a Work with a partner. Think about two methods of communication that animals use.

b Read the text quickly to see if any of your ideas are mentioned.

Talk to the Animals

Only humans speak using words. But all species in the animal kingdom can communicate in one way or another. Maybe you have heard about the way bees dance around to send messages to each other and the way dogs bark in different ways to give warnings, to be friendly or to be playful.

But did you know about infrasonic communication used by elephants? This is how it works:

Humans hear low sounds like the bass notes in music or thunder rumbling in the sky. But we don't hear sounds lower than these. However, animals such as elephants and hippos can hear much lower sounds than humans can. And what's more, they can make sounds in that range as well, and they use them to communicate with each other. This is known as *infrasound*.

Another amazing thing about infrasound is that it travels over several kilometres. Sounds which have a higher pitch, like the ones people can hear, don't travel well through walls, leaves, trees, and so on, which is why we can't hear sounds from more than 100 metres away. But infrasound is much 'stronger', and things like grass and trees have no effect on it. Therefore it can travel much further. Elephants can hear infrasonic calls from four kilometres away!

There have been reports of people watching herds of elephants feeding or resting and then the elephants suddenly all charged off for no reason at all. They obviously heard a warning call from a long way away, but the people didn't hear a sound. In places like a zoo or wildlife park where you can get nearer to animals, it is a bit easier to sense when infrasonic sounds are made. When you stand near mother elephants with their babies in a zoo you may notice a slight rumbling in the air every few minutes – not loud or strong, but clearly noticeable. This is infrasonic communication – the mother elephants 'talking' to their babies!

c ▶ CD1 T14 Read the text again and listen. Circle the correct answer, a, b or c.

1 The writer mentions bees and dogs …
   a because they want to learn how they communicate.
   b as examples of animal communication.
   c because they use infrasonic communication.

2 Humans can hear …
   a lower sounds than elephants can.
   b sounds that travel long distances.
   c sounds with higher pitch.

3 Things like trees …
   a cause problems for low sounds.
   b cause problems for high sounds.
   c don't affect sounds at all.

4 In places like zoos …
   a humans can sense when infrasonic sounds are being made.
   b elephants don't need to make infrasonic sounds.
   c it is easier than in wildlife parks to sense when elephants use infrasonic sounds.

d Read the words from the text and (circle) the correct meaning.

1. animal kingdom
   a. all the living creatures in the world
   b. all living creatures that can communicate

2. warning
   a. a friendly greeting
   b. a message about danger

3. bass
   a. very low
   b. very high

4. rumble
   a. to make long, low sounds
   b. to move quickly and noisily

5. range
   a. the limits between which something is possible
   b. the inside of something

6. pitch
   a. the time a sound lasts
   b. the level of a sound

7. charge off
   a. move away slowly
   b. run away quickly

8. notice
   a. think about
   b. sense

e Use the words from Exercise 10d to complete the sentences.

1. I can't believe you didn't .... that the alarm bell rang.
2. Elephants give a .... to other elephants if they are in danger of attack.
3. Kids can choose from a wide .... of activities at this school – ballet, guitar, etc.
4. He was so angry that he .... without saying goodbye.
5. Animals aren't the only members of the .... Humans are too!
6. I can't hear the elephants. The .... is too low for my ears.

11 Speak

Discuss these questions in small groups.

1. Why is it important for animals to be able to communicate?
2. What difference would it make to the world if animals were able to speak our language?

12 Write

a Read Kylie's composition about a person she has known for a long time. Do they see each other now?

b Kylie uses two tenses in her composition. Which are they? Underline them in different colours.

c Think of a person you have known for a long time. Write about when you first met them and about some things you did together. Use Kylie's composition to help you. Write 120–150 words.

My friend Rebecca

I have known my friend Rebecca for a long time. We first met at a friend's birthday party five years ago. We found out that we both liked techno and Green Day, so I invited Rebecca over to my place. We listened to music together and soon became best friends.

Three years ago, Rebecca's parents invited me to go on holiday with them! It was great. We spent three wonderful weeks in a little cottage in Ireland. Rebecca and I loved walking along the beautiful beach. We took a lot of photos and had a lot of fun.

Two years ago I spent a week in hospital and Rebecca came to see me every day. But then, last year, Rebecca's father changed his job, and they moved to another town. Since then we haven't seen each other very much, but we've talked on the phone and we've written emails to each other.

For your portfolio

3 A true friend

* Past simple vs. past continuous review
* Past simple vs. past perfect simple
* Time conjunctions
* Vocabulary: friends and enemies

1 Speak and read

a How many stories, films, TV programmes or cartoons do you know that involve dogs or other animals?

b Match the phrases with the pictures. Write 1–5 in the boxes.

1. A dog watching over a cot
2. A horse galloping
3. A dog whimpering
4. Someone swinging a sword.
5. A dog greeting his master

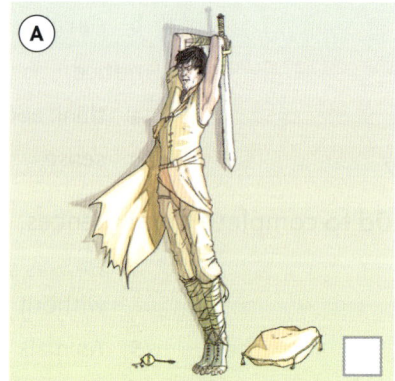
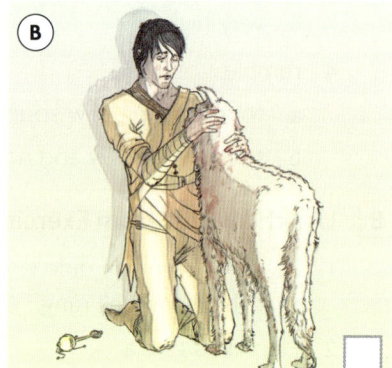

c Work with a partner. Look at the pictures again and put them in order to tell the first part of a story.

d ▶ CD1 T15 Read and listen to the story. Check your ideas from Exercise 1c.

GELERT – The faithful dog

Prince Llewellyn was out hunting on his horse in the Welsh countryside. Back home, his newborn son was sleeping as Gelert, his faithful dog, watched over him. While the Prince and his men were riding through the forest, they heard loud barking coming from the direction of the house. The Prince had a terrible feeling. He turned his horse around and galloped quickly home.

When Prince Llewellyn walked through the door, Gelert was waiting for him. As soon as he saw his master, the dog jumped up to greet him with a huge smile on his face. The Prince looked at Gelert. Something wasn't right. When he looked closer he saw blood dripping from the dog's mouth and fur. Llewellyn ran into his son's bedroom. The cot was empty. The white sheets were covered in blood. The Prince didn't think twice. He took his sword and swung it at the dog. Gelert looked at his master as if he didn't understand. Then with a final whimper, he lay down and died.

e What do you think happened next? How do you think the story ends?

2 Grammar

★ Past simple vs. past continuous review

a Look at these two sentences from the story. Which verbs are in the past simple? Which verbs are in the past continuous?

*While the Prince and his men **were riding** through the forest, they **heard** loud barking coming from the direction of the house.*

*When Prince Llewellyn **walked** through the door, Gelert **was waiting** for him.*

b Complete the rule. Write *past simple*, *past continuous*, *when*, and *while*.

> **RULE:** We use the _____ for an action that happened at one moment in the past. We often use _____ with this tense.
> We use the _____ for a background action or description in the past. We often use _____ with this tense.

c Complete the sentences with the correct form of the verbs.

1. My brother *was climbing* a tree when he *fell* and broke his leg. (climb, fall).
2. When my parents _____ home, we _____ a DVD. (come, watch)
3. Jordan _____ while my sister _____ some homework. (phone, do)
4. While I _____ tennis, a ball _____ me in the eye. (play, hit)
5. Kimberley _____ the web when she _____ a great new site. (surf, find)
6. While we _____ on the beach, it _____ to rain. (walk, start)

★ Time conjunctions: *as / then / as soon as*

d We often use *as*, *then* and *as soon as* when we are talking about the past. Look at these sentences from the story, then complete the box using the words in bold.

***Then** Gelert lay down and died.*

*His newborn son was sleeping **as** Gelert watched over him.*

***As soon as** he saw his master, the dog jumped up to greet him.*

> _____ = at the same time
> _____ = at exactly the same moment
> _____ = the next moment

e Combine the sentences to make a story, using the word in brackets. You may need to change the order of the sentence halves.

1. I left the cinema. I started walking home. (then)

   I left the cinema, then I started walking home.

2. I heard a strange noise. I was walking. (while)
3. I looked up. Something hit me on the head. (as)
4. The thing hit me. Everything went black. (as soon as)
5. I was lying in a hospital bed. I woke up. (when)
6. I rang the bell. A nurse came to talk to me. (as soon as)
7. The nurse was talking to me. I fell in love with her. (while)

f Complete the conversation with the correct form of the verbs.

Alan: Hey Dylan. I hear you played your first concert last night. How was it?

Dylan: It was OK. The audience ¹ *liked* (like) it, I think. But we ² _____ (have) some problems!

Alan: Really? What ³ _____ (happen)?

Dylan: Well, as I ⁴ _____ (sing) the fourth song, all the lights suddenly ⁵ _____ (go) out!

Alan: Oh no! What ⁶ _____ you _____ (do)?

Dylan: The audience sat in the dark and I carried on singing!

Alan: Wow! Well done – that was pretty cool of you.

Dylan: Oh, that was nothing. As soon as the lights ⁷ _____ (come) back on, I realised my microphone ⁸ _____ (not work)! So while the guys ⁹ _____ (fix) the microphone, the band played on, and when it was fixed I ¹⁰ _____ (start) singing again. No problem!

Alan: No problem? Well, I hope all your concerts aren't like that.

Dylan: Yeah – me too!

UNIT 3

3 Speak and read

a Work with a partner. Retell the first part of the story of Gelert.

b ▶ CD1 T16 Read and listen to the second part of the story. What mistake has Llewellyn made?

4 Listen

▶ CD1 T17 Listen to a girl telling the story of Gelert. Write the five things that are different from the story you read.

As Prince Llewellyn looked at his dead dog on the floor he knew that he had done something wrong. He looked around the room and he saw that there had been a fight. There were clothes and broken dishes on the floor. There was a lot more blood too. And then he heard the sound of a baby crying. The noise was coming from under the cot. The Prince slowly lifted it up. There was his baby son, alive and well. On the floor behind the cot he saw the body of a dead wolf. And then the Prince realised. Gelert hadn't killed his son – he had hidden the baby and killed the wolf. Prince Llewellyn was heartbroken. He organised a great ceremony to bury the dog that had saved his son's life. He visited the grave every day until he died.

5 Grammar

✱ Past simple vs. past perfect simple

a Look at these two sentences from the story. Answer the questions.

*He **looked** around the room and he **saw** that there **had been** a fight.*

*He **organised** a great ceremony to bury the dog that **had saved** his son's life.*

1. Did the fight happen when Llewellyn looked around the room or before?
2. What happened first – Llewellyn organised the ceremony or Gelert saved the baby's life?

b Find other examples of the past perfect simple in the story in Exercise 3b, and underline them. Then complete the rule.

> **RULE:** We use the _____ to talk about an event that took place at a particular time in the past.
>
> We use the _____ when we need to make it clear that an event took place <u>before</u> another past event.

c Complete the sentences with the verbs in brackets. One must be in the past perfect simple.

1. When Mike _____ at the station, the train _____ (arrive, leave)
2. The programme _____ when Tessa _____ on the TV. (finish, turn)
3. When they _____ home, the dog _____ their steak. (get, eat)
4. Everybody _____ home when they _____ to the party. (go, get)

d Complete the text with the correct form of the verbs in brackets.

Hidesaburō Ueno was a professor at the University of Tokyo. Every morning his faithful dog Hachikō [1] _____said_____ (say) goodbye to his master at the front door and every evening the dog [2] _____ (go) to Shibuya Station to welcome his master home. One day Professor Ueno [3] _____ (not return) on the usual train. He [4] _____ (have) a heart attack at work and died.

Friends of the Professor [5] _____ (take) the dog to their house to look after him. On the first day when they [6] _____ (arrive) home from work they [7] _____ (find) Hachikō was missing. He [8] _____ (escape) and gone to the station where he [9] _____ (meet) his master so many times. The next day and the day after that Hachikō [10] _____ (do) the same thing. In fact, he continued to meet his master for the next ten years until he finally died too.

Get it right! Turn to page 66.

6 Read and speak

a Read the questionnaire and answer the questions.

b Count how many a, b and c answers you have and check your score on page 71. Do you agree with it?

c Work with a partner. Compare your answers to the questionnaire.

7 Vocabulary

✱ Friends and enemies

Choose the best meaning for the underlined expressions from the questionnaire.

1 <u>let</u> your friend <u>down</u>
   a hit   b disappoint

2 <u>get on well with</u> someone
   a argue a lot
   b have a good relationship with

3 <u>stick up for</u> your friend
   a support   b laugh at

4 <u>fall out with</u> your friend
   a stop being friends with
   b have a fight with

5 <u>tell on</u> your friend
   a talk to
   b tell someone that your friend did something wrong

6 <u>stand by</u> your friend
   a don't speak to
   b be loyal to

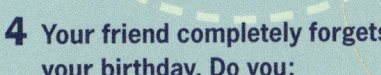 Turn to page 63.

8 Pronunciation

✱ Linking sounds

▶ CD1 T18   Turn to page 62.

9 Speak

Think of another question to test how loyal people are. Work in pairs or small groups and discuss your questions. Use the vocabulary from Exercise 7.

Are you a loyal friend?

Try this quiz and see.

1 **You've promised to meet a friend to go shopping, but another friend has just phoned to invite you to do something better. Do you:**
   a let your first friend down and not go shopping?
   b keep to your original arrangement and go shopping?
   c phone the first friend and explain the situation? You get on well with them, so they will understand.

2 **People are saying that your friend cheated in a test. Do you:**
   a not speak to your friend the next time you see them?
   b stick up for your friend by saying that they would never do anything like that?
   c tell your friend and ask them to explain what happened?

3 **Your friend asks you to lie to their mum about where they were last night. Do you:**
   a tell their mum the truth – you can't lie to your friend's mum?
   b lie for them, of course?
   c ask them why and then decide if you agree with their reasons?

4 **Your friend completely forgets your birthday. Do you:**
   a fall out with your friend – that's the last time you'll speak to them!
   b realise that your friend is probably worried about something else and not make a fuss about it?
   c wait until the next day and then ask your friend why they forgot it?

5 **Your friend has broken one of the school computers. People think it was you. Do you:**
   a tell on your friend, so that they get into trouble, not you?
   b just say you did it and stand by your friend? They would do the same for you.
   c do your best to explain it wasn't you, and hope no one finds out that it was your friend?

UNIT 3   23

What friends are for

10 Read and listen

a ▶ CD1 T19 Who has given Laura flowers and why? Read, listen and check your ideas.

Amy: Hey Laura, I've just got a really exciting email.
Laura: What about?
Amy: It's from RapMan's agent. He's going to play a show in town next month and they're inviting someone from the station to go and interview him. They're also throwing in a ticket to the show.
Laura: Wow, I suppose you're going to take that story then.
Amy: Well, of course I'd love to, but it's on the 16th. That's my mum's birthday and we always go out for dinner somewhere.
Laura: I'll do it.
Amy: Oh, all right. Are you a fan?
Laura: Not especially, but this is too big a story to pass up on! Imagine how many listeners we'll get for this one.
Amy: OK, then. It's yours.

Tom: Hi Laura. You look pretty pleased with yourself.
Laura: As a matter of fact, I am. Amy's just given me the best news story.
Tom: Yeah? So what is it?
Laura: Can you keep a secret?
Tom: I'll try.
Laura: RapMan's in town and I've got a free ticket to his show. And I'm going to interview him! Amy asked me and I said yes.
Tom: RapMan? How could you, Laura?
Laura: What? Why?
Tom: Well, Nick's his biggest fan. He's got all his CDs, posters all over his wall.
Laura: That's news to me.
Tom: Well it's true. I'm sure he'll be going to the show. But if he knew you were going to meet the man himself, he'd be totally envious.
Laura: But he's bound to find out. I'm doing the interview for the radio! I need to talk to him.
Tom: Yes – and the sooner the better!

Tom: Wow. Who's the secret admirer, then?
Laura: What?
Tom: The flowers. Who gave you the flowers?
Laura: Oh, don't be silly. They're from Nick. To say thank you.
Tom: For letting him do the RapMan interview?
Laura: That's right. Did you hear the show? Nick did a much better job of it than I would have.
Tom: Yeah, it was great. And Laura? It was cool of you to let him do it.
Laura: Well, that's what friends are for.

b Answer the questions.

1 Why doesn't Amy go to the Rapman concert and do the interview?
2 Why does Tom say: 'How could you, Laura?'
3 Did Laura know that Nick likes Rapman?
4 Why does Laura need to talk to Nick?
5 What is Tom and Laura's opinion of Nick's report?

11 Everyday English

a Find the expressions 1–6 in the story. Who says them? Match them to the meanings a–f.

1 Not especially, …
2 …, then.
3 As a matter of fact, …
4 How could you?
5 That's news to me.
6 The sooner the better.

a I didn't know that – and I'm surprised.
b That wasn't a good thing to do/say.
c Not really, …
d It's important to do it now – don't wait!
e The fact is, …
f … in that case.

b Complete the dialogue with expressions 1–6 from Exercise 11a.

Paula: Hi Jenny. Where are you going?
Jenny: Hi Paula. I'm going to watch a football match.
Paula: Oh. You like football, ¹ _then_ ?
Jenny: ² _____, but it's the inter-schools competition and my brother Andy's playing, so I'm going along to support him.
Paula: Andy plays football? ³ _____ . I thought he only liked tennis.
Jenny: No, he plays football a bit too. But he's not a good footballer at all. ⁴ _____, he's awful!
Paula: Jenny! ⁵ _____ ?
Jenny: Sorry, it's true! But he could be a really good tennis player. I think he should stop playing football and concentrate on tennis – and ⁶ _____ . Anyway – bye, Paula. Must go or I'll be late for the game!

Discussion box

1 Do you think Laura was right to give the tickets and interview to Nick?
2 Give an example of your own when you wanted to say 'That's what friends are for!'

12 Improvisation

Work in pairs. Take two minutes to prepare a short role play. Try to use some of the expressions from Exercise 11a. Do not write the text, just agree on your ideas for a short scene. Then act it out.

Roles: Nick and Nick's mother or father.
Situation: at home, Nick's room
Basic idea: Nick is doing some homework but is having some problems. His mum/dad asks him how he's getting on.

13 Making Waves ⊙ DVD 3 Episode 1

a 1 Nick, Laura, Amy and Tom are journalists for the school radio station. What kind of stories do you think they report?
2 Do you have a school radio station or magazine? If not, would you like one?

b Match the words with their definitions.

1 to broadcast — d
2 follow a story
3 run a story
4 set up an interview
5 reporter
6 breaking news

a to find out about some news and watch what happens next
b to arrange a meeting with someone so you can ask them questions
c someone who finds news stories
d this is what a radio station does
e a story that has only just happened
f to report a news item

c Watch Episode 1. Who is Amy angry with, and why? Is Nick a good friend to Tom?

14 Write

a Read the story. Where did Adam and Jessica meet? What happened to Jessica?

Jessica and Adam met five years ago. She was working in London[1]. One day she saw him[2]. He was a university student, but was doing a summer job[3]. He had come to the place where she was working[4].

As Adam was leaving, he left a little message next to Jessica's computer[5]. Jessica phoned him[6] and they met the same evening. Adam and Jessica liked each other a lot[7]. One day a terrible thing happened. Jessica was run over by a car[8]. She was badly hurt. Six months later Jessica was OK again. Adam had helped her a lot[9].

For your portfolio

b Answer the questions about Jessica and Adam using your own ideas.

1 What was she working as?
  a programmer for an IT company
2 Where did she see him?
3 What was he working as?
4 Where exactly was she working?
5 What did the message say?
6 When did she phone him?
7 What did they like about each other?
8 What was she doing at that moment?
9 How had Adam helped her?

c Rewrite the story in 120–150 words. Use your answers in Exercise 14b to make the story more interesting. Remember to use linking words like *when* and *while*.

15 Last but not least: more speaking

a Read the first line of each dialogue and match them with the situations in the box.

> Online   An introduction by a friend   At a social or sports club   At a party

1 I don't really know anyone here. I came with my brother but he went home ages ago.
2 Excuse me, is this the right room for the chess club?
3 Hi Sam95. U r right – Beyonce's much better than Rihanna.
4 Laura, this is my best friend Anna. I know you two are going to get on really well.

b What are the advantages and disadvantages of meeting people in the situations in Exercise 15a?

c What other places are good for meeting new people and making friends?

d Talk about friends you have who aren't from your school. Talk about:
- where you met them.
- what your first impressions were.
- why you became friends.
- what it is that you like about them.

Check your progress

1 Grammar

a Complete the sentences. Use the correct form of the past simple or present perfect simple.

1 I *'ve never had* (never have) a surprise party.
2 I _____ (leave) school last June.
3 Why _____ you _____ (not tell) me yesterday?
4 I still _____ (not send) an email to Dave. I'll do it now.
5 How long _____ she _____ (have) that piercing? It looks new.
6 _____ you _____ (go) to the cinema last night? ☐ 5

b Complete the story. Use the correct form of the past simple or past continuous.

A few years ago, when I ¹ *was* (be) a student, I ² _____ (arrange) to meet a friend who ³ _____ (visit) London for a weekend. Unfortunately, I ⁴ _____ (forget) to ask him one very important thing – the full name and address of his hotel. I ⁵ _____ (not have) any way to contact him, so I just ⁶ _____ (decide) to look for him in the busiest street in the city! What ⁷ _____ I _____ (think)? Anyway, I ⁸ _____ (begin) to give up when – you've guessed it – I ⁹ _____ (look) up and ¹⁰ _____ (see) my friend. He ¹¹ _____ (walk) straight towards me, with a big smile on his face. ☐ 10

c Complete the sentences. Use the correct form of the past simple and past perfect.

1 That *was* (be) the first time I *had met* (meet) her.
2 We _____ (not be) hungry because we _____ (eat) lunch already.
3 Everyone _____ (go) to bed when I _____ (get) home.
4 We _____ (arrive) late but luckily the film _____ (not start).
5 They _____ (take) my plate away but I _____ (not finish) eating!
6 _____ Jon _____ (see) the film before? Yes – he _____ (see) it last week. ☐ 10

2 Vocabulary

a Complete the sentences with the verbs in the box.

> ~~gesture~~ lean make nod
> give look fold

1 Why is he *gesturing* at you like that? Have you done something wrong?
2 If you can't hear me, you could _____ forward a little.
3 Just _____ your head if it's too painful to talk.
4 Do I _____ nervous? I feel terrified!
5 I've been trying to _____ eye contact with her for ages, but she's not looking this way.
6 _____ him a warm smile and everything will be fine.
7 When you _____ your arms, does it mean you're upset with me? ☐ 6

b Complete the sentences with the correct form of *say* or *tell*.

1 Have you ever *told* a joke where no one laughed?
2 She never _____ goodbye when she leaves the house.
3 I can't _____ the difference between these computers.
4 I crashed my bike into the wall and my dad really _____ me off.
5 It's never too late to _____ sorry.
6 He didn't even _____ thank you for the present. ☐ 5

How did you do?

Check your score.

Total score	😊 Very good	😐 OK	☹ Not very good
☐ 36			
Grammar	20 – 25	14 – 19	less than 14
Vocabulary	8 – 11	5 – 7	less than 5

4 A working life

* Present perfect simple vs. continuous review
* had better / should / ought to
* Vocabulary: fields of work, jobs and work

1 Vocabulary
Fields of work

a Match the fields of work in the box with the pictures.

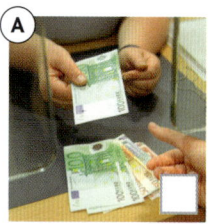   
  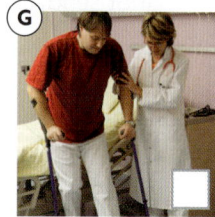 

1 public service
2 education
3 entertainment
4 health care
5 IT and media
6 legal
7 finance
8 management

b Name two jobs for each of the fields of work in Exercise 1a.

2 Read and listen

a Read the blog comments. Which fields do the teenagers want to work in when they're older?

b ▶ CD1 T20 Read the texts again, and listen. <u>Underline</u> the false statement about each person.

1 Abi *hates working at Burger Barn / meets different kinds of people in her job / doesn't want to work at Burger Barn when she's older.*
2 Connor *cycles and delivers newspapers / can afford his own things / is leaving the shop soon.*
3 Tamanna *works for free / wants to do volunteer legal work / believes volunteering will help her to get a paid job.*

Discussion box
1 What are the best part-time jobs in the place where you live?
2 What jobs do you think will exist in fifty years that don't exist now?

What part-time job do you do now? What do you want to do in the future? Leave your comment here!

I've been working at Burger Barn for two months. I thought I'd hate it, but it's been really good. I've learned a lot about how to work with all kinds of people I would never normally meet. And I'm not as shy as I was. I don't think I want to work there forever, but it's given me some ideas about how to run a business. Maybe I'll do business studies when I go to college.

Abi, 15, from York

I've been doing a paper round since last year. I have to get up pretty early so that people can read the news with their breakfast, but I do the round on my bike, so it doesn't take too long. The money isn't great, but I've bought myself a computer with it. They've asked me to work in the shop in the holidays, so that'll be more money. I'm not sure what I want to do in the future. I'm getting good with my computer, so maybe something like programming.

Connor, 14, from Dublin

I've been volunteering at a care home for elderly people on Saturday mornings. Some of my friends think I'm mad, doing a job for no pay, but I really like it. I think that in a few months, I'll try to get a paid part-time job in a solicitor's office because I want to be a lawyer in the future. There's a lot of competition for part-time jobs, but I think my volunteering will look good on my CV.

Tamanna, 16, from London

3 Grammar

✱ Present perfect simple vs. continuous review

a How do we form the present perfect simple and continuous? Read the examples and then complete the rule with *simple* or *continuous*.

I've been working at Burger Barn for two months.
I've learned a lot about how to work with all kinds of people.
I've been doing a paper round since last year.
I've bought myself a computer.

> **RULE:** We use the present perfect _____ to focus on the result of an action. We may also use it to say how often we have done something.
>
> We use the present perfect _____ to focus on an action that started in the past and that may or may not be completed. We may also use it to say how long it is from the start of the action to now.

b Find other examples of the present perfect in the text and underline them.

c Complete the sentences with the verbs in the box.

> written   been playing   read
> been reading   ~~played~~   been writing

1 I'm not surprised the players are tired – they've __played__ four matches this week.
2 My sister's _____ five text messages since breakfast – I wonder who they're to?
3 My fingers hurt! I've _____ emails all morning.
4 I've _____ this page three times already, but I still don't understand it.
5 Can we stop now? We've _____ this game for more than an hour, and I'm bored!
6 I've _____ this book for hours, and I'm still only on page 5.

d Match the questions with the replies. Complete the sentences with the correct form of the verbs in brackets.

1 Do you want a chocolate?
2 Why's your sister so angry?
3 Do you want to watch *Iron Man*?
4 Why's your father so tired?
5 Is it alright if I go out now, Mum?
6 Does your sister speak French?
7 How's the homework going?

a Not very well. I still _____ (not finish).
b No thanks, I __'ve eaten__ (eat) four today already!
c Wait a minute. _____ you _____ (clean) your room?
d Only a little. She _____ (not learn) it for very long.
e She _____ (argue) with her boyfriend all day.
f I don't know. _____ he _____ (work) in the garden?
g OK. Can you believe I _____ (never see) it?

4 Speak

Work with a partner. Take turns to start a new conversation.

Tell your partner about:

- your favourite piece of clothing
- something you are learning/ studying
- the place where you live
- a book you are reading
- a good friend of yours who is not in your class

Your partner asks you questions:

How long ...? (have it)
How long ...? (learn/study it)
How long ...? (live there)
How long ...? (read it)
How long ...? (know them)

> **LOOK!**
> *have* (= possess) and *know* are not normally used in the continuous form.
> *I have known her for three years.*
> (Not: *I have been knowing her for three years.*)

5 Pronunciation

✱ /ɔː/ *short*

▶ CD1 T21 and T22   Turn to page 62.

6 Listen

a Look at the list of some popular part-time jobs for teenagers in the UK and the USA. What questions do you think you might have to answer at an interview for these jobs?

shop assistant   supermarket shelf stacker   babysitter   waiter
cinema usher   barista   petsitter   video game tester   homework tutor

b ▶ CD1 T23 Listen to the conversation between Chloe and Ryan. What job did Ryan have an interview for? Do you think he got the job?

c ▶ CD1 T23 Listen again. Which questions did Ryan have to answer in his interview? Tick (✔) the ones you hear.

1. How did you hear about the job?
2. Did you see our advertisement?
3. What experience do you have?
4. What hours can you work?
5. Can you speak another language?
6. Why do you want to work for us?
7. How much money do you want to earn?
8. Can you fill in an application form?

d ▶ CD1 T23 How did Ryan answer the questions? Listen again to check.

7 Grammar

★ *had better / should / ought to*

a Look at the examples from the conversation in Exercise 6b, then complete the rule using the words in bold.

1. You **should** be more serious at an interview.
2. I said I was useless in the mornings, so they'**d better** give me afternoons …
3. You **ought to** go back and say sorry.

> **RULE:** We use _____ or _____ to give general advice and opinions. They have a similar meaning.
>
> We use _____ to give advice for a specific situation. There is the idea that there will be a problem if the advice is not followed. It is always used in the past form.

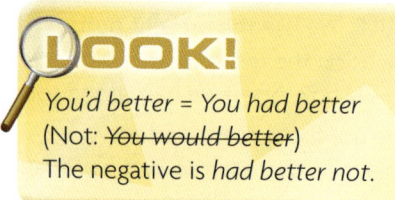

You'd better = You had better
(Not: *You would better*)
The negative is *had better not*.

b Complete the sentences with the correct form of *should*, *ought to* or *had better*.

1. I've got an exam tomorrow. I think I'd _better_ get a good night's sleep.
2. Your hair looks terrible – you _____ to go to the hairdresser's.
3. Listen, it's really late. I think we _____ leave soon.
4. I'm not surprised she's angry – you _____ talk to people in that way!
5. OK, you can borrow my camera – but you'd _____ lose it!
6. If you want a good career, you _____ to work harder at school!

c Work with a partner. Decide what answers Ryan from Exercise 6b should give next time he has an interview.

8 Speak

Work with a partner. Take turns giving your partner advice. Student B: turn to page 71.

Student A: Ask your partner for advice about these problems.

You have a big test tomorrow and you haven't studied for it.

You borrowed a DVD from a friend, but you sat on it and broke it by accident.

You don't want to go on holiday with your parents this year.

Now think of your own problem.

30 UNIT 4

9 Vocabulary

★ Jobs and work

a ▶ CD1 T24 Match the definitions 1–10 with the words and expressions a–j. Then listen, check and repeat.

1. to write a letter to ask for a job
2. a person who works for a company
3. a person or company that gives people a job
4. to have a job for 35–40 hours a week
5. to have a job for a few hours a week
6. official records showing you have finished a training course or you have skills
7. to say that you want to leave a job
8. the money you get paid every month for doing your job
9. a person who is learning how to do a job
10. not having a job / out of work

a. work full-time
b. unemployed
c. work part-time
d. trainee
e. resign
f. salary
g. employee
h. apply for a job
i. qualifications
j. employer

b Complete the questions using expressions from Exercise 9a.

1. A: Is your job ___full-time___ ?
   B: Yes, I work 40 hours a week.
2. A: Is he still _____ ?
   B: Yes, he has been out of work for two years.
3. A: Are you on a good _____ ?
   B: Not really. I only get £400 a month.
4. A: Why did you _____ this job?
   B: Because I thought it seemed really interesting.
5. A: Why did he _____ ?
   B: Because he found a better job with another company.
6. A: Is your job _____ ?
   B: Yes, I only work twelve hours a week.
7. A: How many _____ have you got?
   B: More than 400. And they're doing a good job.
8. A: Do you have any _____ ?
   B: Yes, I passed my teaching exams in 2009.
9. A: Who was your last _____ ?
   B: I worked for British Airways.
10. A: Did you work here first as a _____ ?
    B: Yes. They give you a year to learn how to do the job.

Get it right! Turn to page 67.

10 Listen

▶ CD1 T25 Listen to the job interview and make notes under the headings.

Job wanted   Experience
Current job   Qualifications

11 Speak

Work with a partner. Choose one of the jobs from the advertisements and roleplay a job interview. One of you is the interviewer, the other wants the job. Use language from Exercise 9. Then choose a different job and swap roles. Think about:

reasons for application (Why / apply?)

qualifications (What kind of qualifications / have?)

work experience (What kind of work experience / have?)

expected salary (What salary / expect?)

New TV show requires animal trainer

Rock band looking for singer

Youth Representative Local government wants to hear what

Writers needed for online arts magazine

UNIT 4   31

Fiction in mind

12 Read and listen

a Think of four reasons why someone might not be happy in their job.

b Read the extract. Chester is not completely happy in his job. Why not?

The Book of Thoughts by Frank Brennan

The story so far:
Chester is a young man with a good job in Singapore. But Chester doesn't know who he can trust at work, and he needs to know. Then one day he stops at an antique book store on his way home …

Chester was feeling more tired than usual after a hard day at the office. He had joined the company only two years before. He had come straight from university then, but now he was a junior manager in one of the biggest companies in Singapore. It was an important position to have and meant lots of extra work.

He could understand the jealousy that some of the other workers might feel against the 'new boy', as they still called him. He had risen quickly in the company. Many of them, however, had been there for years doing the same job. He could understand how bad feelings towards him might lie behind their smiles.

But it didn't make life any easier.

He needed people whose advice he could trust when he had to make difficult decisions. He had to be sure that the bad feelings of the other workers didn't get in the way of the important business decisions he had to make. He knew he would never become a manager unless he could be sure of people.

Then there was Dorothy. […]

Ah, Dorothy!

Take today, for example. He had been given some new figures to check and he had asked Dorothy to read some of the details to him while he took notes. It was not until she had left that he realised that he had not written notes at all. Instead he had written Dorothy's name several times. He was too embarrassed to ask Dorothy for the details again, so he had to look them up in the office of old Mr Shaw.

Mr Shaw was always known for being in a bad mood and he was no different this time. He didn't like having to stay late to check figures for some junior manager. He didn't like it at all.

Chester hated it when he made mistakes. It didn't look good. But it didn't happen often.

He decided he would walk home instead of taking the train. It was late in the evening but he felt he needed the walk to clear his thoughts after a busy day. Anyway, it would be a little punishment for being so stupid earlier on. He decided that he would eat at the shopping centre near his home. […]

As he walked towards his favourite Chinese restaurant, he saw that the lights were still on in an old antique shop. […] There were boxes of old books piled outside the shop. […]

There was one small, old book that he noticed at once. It looked much older than the rest of the books. He picked it up.

'Take it!' said a voice behind him.

c ▶ CD1 T26 Read the extract again and listen. Answer the questions.

1. Why does Chester think that other people in the company have 'bad feelings' towards him?
2. Why is it important for Chester to 'be sure of people'?
3. How does Chester feel about Dorothy?
4. Why doesn't Chester like making mistakes?
5. Why does Chester decide to walk home?

d The book in the antique shop has special powers. What can the book do, do you think? (Think about the title of the story!)

Discussion box

What do you think is the most important thing for someone to be happy in their job?

UNIT 4

13 Write

a Read Sophie's job application. What job is she applying for?

b Read the letter again and answer the questions.

1. Where does Sophie write her name, and where does she write her address?
2. Where does she put the date?
3. How does she start the main part of the letter? What do you write if you know the name of the person you are writing to, for example *Richard Clark* or *Deborah Jenkins*?
4. In which paragraph does she say what her reason for writing is?
5. How does she organise her reasons for believing that she is the right person for the job?
6. How does she end the letter? What do you write if you know the name of the person you are writing to?

123 South Street
Rochester
Kent ME8 7BY
Tel: 01889 389456
solake@freespace.co.uk

HR Department
e-Style
Romsey Street
Birmingham B60 3DH

23 June, 2010

Dear Sir

I read your advertisement for a web designer in yesterday's *Times* and would like to apply. I enclose my CV as requested. I think there are several reasons why I might be the right person for the job.

First of all, I have always been fascinated by technology. I got my first computer when I was eight, and I have been interested in the internet since then. I created my own website at the age of 14, and since then I have been designing websites for my friends.

Secondly, I believe I have the right qualifications. I have taken several courses in IT, including specialist courses in Java and Flash. I was an assistant for a web design studio for six weeks during the summer holidays. I have been working part-time for the same studio since then, as well as being a student.

Lastly, I would like to stress that I would love to work in a team with other people who have more experience than me. I would love to improve my skills through learning from others. I am very willing to work hard, and I do not mind working overtime.

I can be contacted by phone or email for an interview. I look forward to hearing from you.

Yours faithfully

Sophie Lake

Sophie Lake

c Write a letter of application for one of the jobs in Exercise 11. Remember to say which job you are applying for and where you saw the advertisement. Use Sophie's letter to help you. Write 120–150 words.

5 Live forever!

* Future predictions
* First conditional review: *if* and *unless*
* Vocabulary: time conjunctions, verbs with prepositions

1 Read and speak

a Ray Kurzweil is one of 18 great modern thinkers who are trying to solve some of the world's biggest challenges. Here are some of the problems they are considering.

1. making solar energy much cheaper ☐
2. getting clean water to everyone ☐
3. improving towns and cities ☐
4. developing virtual reality technology ☐
5. improving health care and medicine ☐

Put them in order of importance for you.

b Read the text. Which of the problems in Exercise 1a does it mention?

c Match the titles with the paragraphs. Write A–E in the boxes. There is one title you won't use.

A Medical advances
B Fun in the future
C Who wants to live forever?
D Bigger and better brains
E Solutions to the Earth's problems

d ▶ CD1 T27 Listen and check your answers.

Discussion box

1. If you were one of the 18 great thinkers, which problems would you discuss?
2. Imagine you are going to live to the age of 200. What are you going to do to stop yourself from getting bored?

1 ☐ If Ray Kurzweil is right, this is a question we'll have to ask ourselves in the near future. Kurzweil is an inventor and futurist with some interesting ideas on how humans will soon be able to live much longer than the average 78 years they do now.

2 ☐ The first challenge is how to stop our bodies from getting old and dying. Kurzweil doesn't see this as a problem. With gene technology we'll soon be able to 'turn off' genes that cause ageing and disease. This technology is getting cheaper and advancing at an incredible rate. Kurzweil believes that from every year after 2023, we'll be adding more than a year to the average life expectancy. He also expects that within the next 20 years, we will have 'nanobots' in our blood. These tiny robots will automatically keep our bodies healthy and free from diseases by finding damaged cells and destroying them.

3 ☐ Of course, if we're all going to live longer, then there are going to be more of us on this already overcrowded Earth. Many people think there are likely to be problems with resources such as food and energy. Kurzweil doesn't agree. He says that the same technologies used to increase our life expectancy will also be used to help with food production and energy needs. For example, he says, sunlight can potentially give us 10,000 times more energy than we currently use. We just need to develop the technology to capture it and make it cheaper. There are also new technologies that can recycle water extremely cheaply. This means that dirty water can be made clean again at a very low cost. When you consider that 80% of disease in the developing world is because of dirty water, you can see how this technology might help change the world.

4 ☐ But what are we going to do with all this extra time? Won't we all get bored? Again Kurzweil says 'no'. For a start, we won't be stuck in old bodies. We'll stay young for years. This will mean we'll be able to experiment with many more things than we can now. We'll also see huge developments in virtual reality technology that will keep us entertained for years.

The future according to Ray Kurzweil looks good – and we might just be around to see it.

34 UNIT 5

2 Grammar
✱ Future predictions

a Look at the text on page 34 and complete the sentences.

1. Many people think there _____ be problems with resources such as food and energy.
2. For a start, we _____ be stuck in old bodies.
3. Huge developments in virtual reality technology _____ keep us entertained for years.
4. The future according to Ray Kurzweil looks good and we _____ just be around to see it.

b Complete the list with the words in the box.

> ~~will~~   will probably   ~~isn't likely to~~   won't
> might not   probably won't   is likely to   ~~might~~

100% ↑
The chance of something happening
↓ 0%

1. *will*
2. _____ _____
3. *might*
4. _____
5. _____ *isn't likely to*
6. _____

c Decide if the speaker in these situations is sure or not sure. Write *'ll*, *won't*, *might* or *might not*.

1. A: I'm going to Disneyland in Paris next week.
   B: Oh, you _____ love it. I went there last year and it was wonderful.
2. A: Are you coming to the party tonight?
   B: Actually, I _____ . I want to, but I have to get up early tomorrow. Ask me again later.
3. A: Do you know where you're going for your holidays next year?
   B: We _____ go to South Africa. We haven't really decided yet, though.
4. A: Can I have the last piece of pizza?
   B: If you do, there _____ be any left for your brother!

d Rewrite the sentences using the word in brackets.

1. She's always late so she's not likely to arrive before nine. (probably)
   She probably won't arrive before nine.
2. He'll get to the tennis final but he probably won't win. (likely)
3. Tomorrow's a holiday so the traffic is likely to be bad. (probably)
4. He hasn't studied at all so he'll probably fail the test. (likely)
5. The weather forecast says it's not likely to rain tomorrow. (probably)

e Work with a partner and make predictions about these subjects.

1. Scientists will bring dinosaurs back to life.
   A: *That isn't likely to happen.*
   B: *I think it might happen.*
2. Men will give birth to babies.
3. Your country will win the next World Cup.
4. We'll discover life on other planets.
5. You'll pass the end-of-year exams.
6. You'll get married before you're 20.
7. You'll find the perfect partner.
8. You'll have four or more children.

UNIT 5

3 Listen and speak

a How old is the oldest person you know?

b Look at the items in the box. Say which things you think help people to live longer, and which things don't help. Explain why to a partner.

doing exercise   being optimistic
having a pet   relaxing
choosing the right partner
happiness   eating well
money   laughter   sleep
learning new things   friendship

c ▶ CD1 T28 Listen to the first part of a radio show about longevity with people talking about what they think will help them to live longer. Which items in the box are mentioned?

4 Grammar

★ First conditional review: *if* and *unless*

a ▶ CD1 T28 Listen again and circle the correct words in the sentences.

1 *You'll always be / You always are* worried, if *you'll be / you are* short of money.
2 *I'll hopefully live / I hopefully live* to a good age, if *I keep / I'll keep* doing these exercises.
3 If *I'll always have / I always have* good friends around me, *I'll live / I live* to be 100.
4 Unless *you look / will look* for the good things in life, *you'll never be / you are never* happy.

b Read the rule and circle the correct words.

> **RULE:**
> 1 In these sentences, both verbs refer to actions or events *in the present / in the present or future*.
> 2 The verb tense after the words *if* or *unless* is *present simple / a future form*.
> 3 The verb tense in the other clause is *present simple / a future form*.

c Complete the sentences with the verbs in the box.

'll email   leave   won't call   'll fall
won't get   aren't   want   want

1 You *'ll fall* if you _____ careful.
2 Unless we _____ the house right now, we _____ there for the start of the film.
3 I _____ you the photos if you _____.
4 I _____ you at the weekend – unless you _____ me to.

d Make sentences from these words.

1 if / you go near that dog / bite you
   If you go near that dog, it'll bite you.
2 unless / come and eat your pizza now / not be any left
3 if / you are tired / I do the washing-up
4 unless / slow down / crash the car
5 if / buy you a new bike / pass all your exams

5 Listen

▶ CD1 T29 Listen to the second part of the radio show, and circle the correct answer a, b or c.

1 Jeanne Louise Calment holds the world record for
   a being the oldest living person.   b being the oldest Frenchwoman.   c having the longest life.
2 The previous oldest person was
   a 112.   b 118.   c 120.
3 She didn't have a very stressful life because
   a she had plenty of money.   b her husband helped her a lot.   c she was very active.
4 Jeanne Louise Calment believed that chocolate
   a wasn't healthy.   b helped her to live longer.   c didn't harm her.
5 The presenter believes the real reason why Jeanne Louise lived so long was because she
   a came from a good family.   b enjoyed chocolate.   c loved her life.

6 Vocabulary

✱ Time conjunctions: if / unless / when / until / as soon as

a Complete the sentences with the words in the box.

> unless   if   ~~when~~   until   as soon as

1 She was still riding a bike ……*when*…… she was 100.
2 Most doctors agree that ……………… you start smoking, you're creating future health problems.
3 He never did any exercise ……………… his doctor told him to.
4 ……………… your parents and grandparents live to be old, you're more likely to have a long life yourself.
5 ……………… you're happy with your life, you probably won't want to live until you're 100.

b (Circle) the correct words.

1 A: We'll be here all night *when / unless* you do something
   B: There's nothing I can do. We'll stay here *until / if* someone rescues us.

2 A: I want to keep it a secret. *If / As soon as* you see Joey, don't tell him anything.
   B: OK, I won't say anything *unless / as soon as* you change your mind.

3 A: Have you heard? Sarah's going to leave her boyfriend *as soon as / until* he gets back from holiday.
   B: No way! He's going to be so upset *when / if* he finds out.

4 A: Can you ask him to phone me, please? I'll be in my office *if / until* 5.30.
   B: Certainly! I'll tell him *as soon as / unless* he comes back from lunch.

✱ Verbs with prepositions

c Complete these causes of stress using *with*, *for* or *about*.

1 arguing ……………… your parents
2 revising ……………… exams
3 thinking ……………… what to wear
4 worrying ……………… life

d Complete the sentences. Use a verb and preposition from Exercise 6c.

1 I got into trouble today. It wasn't a good idea to ……………… the teacher!
2 She's always happy and smiling – she never seems to ……………… anything!
3 Sorry, I can't come out tonight. There's a test tomorrow and I need to ……………… it.
4 It's time to plan the party. We need to ……………… who to invite!

Vocabulary bank   Turn to page 64.

Get it right!   Turn to page 67.

7 Speak

a Work with a partner. Discuss how stressful the things in Exercise 6c are. Give each one a mark from 0 (not at all) to 5 (extremely).

b In groups, discuss what you find stressful in life. Give each other ideas on how to make these things less stressful.

8 Pronunciation

✱ Prepositions

▶ CD1 T30   Turn to page 62.

UNIT 5   37

9 Listen and speak

a You are going to listen to a song called *Live Forever*. Discuss with a partner ways in which it might be possible for a rock star to 'live forever'. Think of famous dead pop stars to support your ideas.

b ▶ CD1 T31   Listen to the song. Eight words are wrong. Write the correct words.

[1] Maybe (a)I don't really want to know
How your garden grows
Cos (b)I just want to try
Lately did you ever feel the shame
In the morning rain
As it soaks you to the bone?

[2] Maybe I just want to fly
I want to live I don't want to cry
Maybe I just want to sing
Maybe I just don't belong
Maybe you're the same as me
(c)We see things they'll never see
(d)You and I are gonna live forever

Repeat 1

Maybe I will never be
All the people that I want to be
(e)Now is not the time to die
Now's the time to find out why
(f)I think you're the same as them
We see things they'll never see
You and I are gonna live forever

Repeat 1 + 2

c Read this interpretation of the song and match the points (1–6) with the lines from the song (a–f).

I think this song shows perfectly what it's like to be a teenager:

1 They don't think they will ever die.   **d**
2 They like to try out new things. ☐
3 They aren't interested in older people's lives. ☐
4 They don't waste time with regrets. ☐
5 They like to feel they are the same as their friends. ☐
6 They think they know more about the world than older people. ☐

d Discuss the questions in pairs.

Do you agree with the points made about teenagers in Exercise 9c?

What do you think the song is about? Use lines from the song to support your ideas.

Did you know?

Live Forever was the third single that Oasis released from their first album *Definitely Maybe* and it was the song that helped them become one of the world's biggest bands. It was their first top ten hit in the UK and reached number two in the US. The song was written by guitarist Noel Gallagher as a response to the pessimistic atittude of grunge bands that were popular at the time, such as Nirvana and Pearl Jam. Noel wrote the song before he was in the band and when he played it to his brother Liam, he liked it so much he invited Noel to join his band. Noel left Oasis in 2009 after an argument with Liam at a music festival in France.

10 Write

a Read the text quickly to find out if the writer agrees or disagrees with the scientists.

Will computers ever be more intelligent than people?

(a) Scientists claim that, in 50 years' time, there will be computers that are as intelligent as, or even more intelligent than, humans. This is a fascinating idea, but I don't believe it will really happen.

(b) It's true that computer scientists have made some fantastic inventions over the last few years. They have implanted tiny chips in people's brains to help patients with Parkinson's disease. They have developed computers that can understand many things that people say, and can give a meaningful answer most of the time. They have built computers that have enormous memory capacities.

(c) But human intelligence is more than having a good memory. It may be possible to build computers that can remember a lot more than the best human brain. But humans can do a lot more. They laugh and cry, they enjoy a good film or an interesting book.

(d) In conclusion, I would say that in 50 years' time, we will probably have computers that can do all sorts of things that today we cannot even dream of. But I believe human intelligence will always be higher than artificial intelligence.

b Read the text again. Which paragraph:
1 develops one side of the argument?
2 gives the opposing argument?
3 sums up the writer's main ideas?
4 says what the writer is writing about?

c What is the purpose of the underlined sentences in the text?

d Write your own text about one of the following topics.

Will there still be schools and teachers in the future?
Will it be possible to live forever?

Write 120–150 words. Use the organisation of the text in Exercise 10a to help you.

11 Last but not least: more speaking

a When do you think these things will happen? Number the predictions 1–4.

1 Sometime in the near future.
2 Sometime in the next fifty years.
3 One day but not in my lifetime.
4 Never.

a There will be no more wars.
b People will go on holiday to Mars.
c Aliens will live with humans on Earth.
d People will live to an average age of 120.
e Time travel will be common.
f There will be underwater cities.

b Compare your ideas with a partner. Then think of one prediction for each of the time frames in Exercise 11a and discuss your ideas in class.

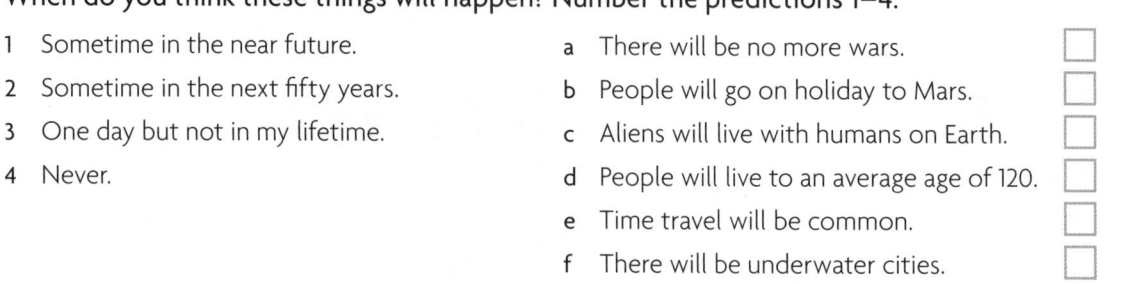

Check your progress

1 Grammar

a Complete the sentences. Use the correct form of the present perfect simple or continuous.

1. Sorry! How long _have_ you _been waiting_ (wait) for me?
2. I _____ (write) ten emails this morning.
3. _____ you _____ (see) my keys anywhere?
4. I _____ (not learn) Japanese very long, but I know lots of words already.
5. Have you looked outside? It _____ (snow) for the last hour.
6. I _____ (not rent) any movies for a month. [5]

b Complete the sentences. Use the correct form of the first conditional.

1. It _won't work_ (not work) unless you _switch_ (switch) it on!
2. I _____ (call) you as soon as I _____ (get) home.
3. If you _____ (not come) inside now, you _____ (miss) the programme.
4. They _____ (not let) you in if you _____ (not be) over 18. [3]

c Rewrite the sentences using the word in brackets.

1. It's really cold, but I don't think it will snow. (likely) It's really cold, but _it isn't likely to snow._
2. Maybe I'll stay in tonight. (might) I _____
3. I don't think I'll finish this today. (probably) I _____
4. He'll probably be hungry when he gets home. (likely) He _____ [3]

2 Vocabulary

a Complete the sentences with words about work.

1. When you haven't got a job, you're _unemployed_
2. Someone who works for a newspaper, for instance, works in the _____ field.
3. If you work _____, you do about 40 hours a week.
4. A degree certificate is an example of a _____
5. If you are paid for singing, dancing, acting or being funny, you work in _____
6. Doctors and nurses work in _____
7. You _____ if you decide to leave a job.
8. The _____ gives you a job.
9. If your business is money, you work in _____
10. What your teacher gives you is _____ [9]

b Circle the correct word.

1. I'll tell you (as soon as) / until I know
2. I can't borrow the car when / unless Dad changes his mind.
3. Please stay until / unless the film is over.
4. Oh no! Mum will be really angry if / when she gets home.
5. Unless / If it's really cold, we won't have the picnic. [4]

c Complete the sentences with *about*, *for* or *with*.

1. Don't argue _with_ me! I'm always right.
2. Don't worry _____ life – just be happy!
3. I'm thinking _____ what present to buy.
4. Are you getting ready _____ the match?
5. Shouldn't you be revising _____ your exam? [4]

How did you do?

Check your score.

Total score	😊 Very good	😐 OK	🙁 Not very good
28			
Grammar	7 – 11	3 – 6	less than 3
Vocabulary	13 – 17	9 – 12	less than 9

UNIT 5

6 Reality TV

* make / let / be allowed to
* Modal verbs of obligation, prohibition and permission
* Vocabulary: television, extreme adjectives and modifiers, making new friends

1 Speak and read

a What do you watch on TV, and what do you watch on a PC?

b What are the most popular reality TV shows in your country? What kind of things do people do on these shows?

c Read the text quickly. Are any of your ideas mentioned?

d ▶ CD1 T32 Read the text again and listen. Answer the questions.

1 Which of these are not mentioned as prizes?
   a money
   b a big house
   c a theatre role
   d a job
   e a restaurant

2 According to the text, which of these activities do participants in *The Amazing Race* not do?
   a take flights
   b do puzzles
   c control animals
   d work in teams
   e dance

3 Which of these is not a reason for the popularity of *The Amazing Race*, according to the text?
   a There are a lot of surprises.
   b Some teams have bad arguments.
   c The team members don't know each other well.
   d The contestants' reactions to problems are realistic.
   e The teams face stressful situations.

Ever fancied being on TV?

The good news is that there's probably a show for you. You could sing and dance to get a part in a musical. You could become an apprentice footballer at a top club, or an apprentice business executive. If you can cook, you might win your own restaurant, or you could invent something amazing and get rich. If you don't actually know how to do anything, you could just let viewers watch you live in a big house, and hope you are voted the most popular resident.

There are more exciting shows, though. How about a race around the world for $1 million? In the US show *The Amazing Race*, eleven pairs of contestants race around the world and have to complete different tasks on the way. These include the 'ordinary' (playing volleyball, gathering sheep), the 'personal' (getting tattooed, shaving your head), the 'disgusting' (eating two kilos of meat, drinking blood), and the 'dangerous' (rolling over in a car, bungee jumping). The pairs are allowed to decide how to get to their destinations — by car, train, boat, plane or bus — but they are not allowed to ask for help or use mobile phones.

This kind of show is not exactly new, so what makes us keep watching? Well, what is different about *The Amazing Race* is that the participants know each other. There are married couples, dating couples, ex-couples, best friends and family members. Just like in real life, people who are close argue and get frustrated with each other when they are stressed. This is what makes the show successful. The contestants (and sometimes the producers) don't know exactly what's going to happen next. Some pairs really come together in these situations, while others completely fall apart. Which is all a little more real than most 'reality' shows.

Discussion box

1 What is good and bad about reality shows? Why do you think reality shows have been so popular?

2 Would you like to be a contestant on a reality TV show? Why / Why not?

2 Grammar
★ make / let / be allowed to

a Look at the text on page 42 and complete the sentences.

1 You could just _____ you live in a big house.
2 The pairs _____ how to get to their destinations.
3 They _____ _____ help or use mobile phones.
4 So what _____ watching?

b (Circle) the correct option to complete the rule.

> **RULE:** We use *be allowed to* to talk about *obligation / permission*.
>
> We use *not be allowed to* to talk about *prohibition / obligation*.
>
> We use *let* to talk about *obligation / permission*.
>
> We use *make* to talk about *obligation / permission*.

c Complete the sentences with the correct form of *make*, *let* or *be allowed to*.

1 At school, we __are__ not __allowed to__ take our mobile phones into the classroom.
2 _____ your teachers _____ you study hard?
3 I never _____ people use my things without asking me first.
4 When I lend things to my brother, I always _____ him promise to look after them!
5 _____ you _____ use your mum's car?
6 I _____ go to bed later at the weekend.
7 Joanna's bought a new CD, and yesterday she _____ me borrow it.
8 Last Saturday, my parents _____ me go shopping with them – it was really boring!

3 Speak

Work in pairs. Ask and answer questions about the rules you have at home. Talk about:

> doing housework   times you can come home
> homework   watching TV   friends visiting you
> listening to music in your room   using the phone
> eating at the table with your family

A: *Are you allowed to listen to music in your room?*
B: *Yeah, but after 11 o'clock at night they make me use headphones. Do your parents make you …?*

4 Vocabulary
★ Television

Complete the text with the words in the box.

> series   contestant   celebrities
> presenter   viewing figures   episode
> audience   viewers   sitcoms   ~~show~~

Did you know that the popular quiz [1] __show__ *Who Wants to be a Millionaire?* started on British TV? Each week, the [2] _____ asks questions on general knowledge, and the [3] _____ has to answer them to try to win a million pounds. There is an [4] _____ in the TV studio, and the programme gets millions of [5] _____ at home too.

Detective [6] _____ are also very popular in Britain, and so are soap operas. A soap opera tells a story about ordinary people, and there is usually something dramatic in each [7] _____ .
[8] _____ like *Friends* also tell a story, but are much funnier than soaps. They usually get very high [9] _____ , sometimes 10 million people or more. The stars often become [10] _____ .

5 Pronunciation
★ /aʊ/ all<u>ow</u>ed

▶ CD1 T33 and T34   Turn to page 62.

UNIT 6

6 Listen and speak

a You are going to listen to a radio show about fame. Look at some of the questions from the radio show. Discuss possible answers with a partner.

1. What percentage of teens say they want to be famous?
2. What do you want to be famous for?
3. Why don't you want to be famous?
4. Do you agree that fame brings problems?

b ▶ CD1 T35 Listen to the radio show. How do the speakers answer the questions in Exercise 6a?

U Got What It Takes?

Come and audition for your place in the nation's biggest talent show. Singers, dancers, musicians …

all welcome!

c ▶ CD1 T35 Listen again. Mark the sentences *T* (true), *F* (false) or *N* (not enough information).

1. Heather does not understand why someone would not want to be famous.
2. A lot of teenagers told Chris Taylor that they didn't care what they were famous for.
3. Jake thinks that people who win reality TV shows deserve to be famous.
4. Jake does not like Britney Spears.
5. Heather doesn't think it is hard to deal with the problems of fame.
6. Chris thinks people who become famous quickly stay famous for longer.

d Work with a partner.

1. Make a list of ways people can become famous.
2. What should people do (or not do) if they want to stay famous?

7 Grammar

★ **Modal verbs of obligation, prohibition and permission**

a Look at these examples from the radio show in Exercise 6b.

*They think you **don't have to** have a reason.*
*They think they **can** do anything they want.*
*Teenagers **mustn't** think that becoming famous is easy.*
*You **have to** practise a lot.*

Match the words in bold with their meaning.

1. something is allowed
2. it is very important not to do something
3. something isn't necessary
4. something is necessary

b Match the sentences with the pictures. Write 1–6 in the boxes.

1. You can wash your hands in there.
2. You have to turn off your phone in here.
3. Great! We don't have to pay.
4. Sorry, you can't go on this ride.
5. You mustn't leave your seat yet.
6. You must be over 18 to get in.

c Complete the sentences with a modal verb.

1. Hurry up – we __mustn't__ be late!
2. Listen everybody – you _____ finish your project by next week. No excuses!
3. Your computer's broken? Don't worry – you _____ use mine.
4. It's Anna's birthday on Friday – I _____ remember to buy a present for her.
5. This is an exam, so sorry – you _____ use your dictionary.
6. If you got all of this exercise correct, you _____ do the homework – you can relax instead!

UNIT 6

8 Vocabulary

★ Extreme adjectives and modifiers

a Look at these sentences from the radio show in Exercise 6b. What do *fantastic*, *huge* and *awful* mean?

*I'm an absolutely **fantastic** singer!*
*Britney Spears is a **huge** star, right?*
*I'd hate that – it must be really **awful**.*

b Match the adjectives 1–10 with the extreme adjectives a–j.

1	big	a	great/fantastic/wonderful/excellent/brilliant
2	small	b	enormous/huge
3	tired	c	boiling
4	hot	d	exhausted
5	cold	e	tiny
6	good	f	starving
7	hungry	g	awful/terrible
8	bad	h	fascinating
9	interesting	i	hilarious
10	funny	j	freezing

c Here are some more sentences from the radio show.

*People are waiting for you to do something **really stupid**.*

*Well, firstly, I think Jake and Heather are **absolutely right** about the problems of fame.*

*For most people it takes a lot of **very hard work** ...*

Look at these examples of adjectives with the modifiers *really*, *very* and *absolutely*. Some you can use together and some you can't. Write a tick (✔) or a cross (✘) beside each one.

- really good ☐
- really great ☐
- really hot ☐
- really boiling ☐
- very good ☐
- very great ☐
- very hot ☐
- very boiling ☐
- absolutely good ☐
- absolutely great ☐
- absolutely hot ☐
- absolutely boiling ☐

I love the Twilight books – they're fascinating.

d Complete the sentences with one of the adjectives in Exercise 8b. There may be more than one answer.

1 I burned my hand. That water was absolutely ___boiling___.
2 Let's go and get some food – I'm very _____.
3 I stayed up all night working. I'm really _____.
4 My puppy is only a week old. It's still really _____.
5 Can I close the window? It's really _____ in here.
6 She told us an absolutely _____ story.
7 That joke is very _____.
8 I hated that programme. It was really _____.

Vocabulary bank Turn to page 64.

9 Speak

Work with a partner. Talk about these topics using the vocabulary from Exercise 8.

films you've seen   holidays you've been on
books you've read   websites you've used

The special effects in *Avatar* are absolutely fantastic.

We were really exhausted after a great holiday in London.

I saw a really awful singer on the internet. It was absolutely hilarious!

Culture in mind

10 Read and speak

a Look at the websites on this page. Do you use any of them? Why are they so popular? What are the problems of using these sites?

Social networks

TV is so 20th century! More and more young people are using online social networks like *mySpace* and *facebook.com*, popular in many different countries. But they're not the only ones. People love ... *friendster* in Indonesia and Malaysia, *orkut* in Brazil, Japan and India, *vkontakte* in Russia, *skyrock* in France, *51.com* in China, *perfspot* in Iran, *cyworld* in South Korea, *bebo* in Ireland and New Zealand, *badoo* in Uruguay.

b Work with a partner. How much do you know about your schoolmates? Will you remember everybody after you leave school? What information would you like to know about them? How could you get it?

c Read about myYearbook.com. Are any of your ideas from Exercise 10b mentioned?

d ▶ CD1 T36 Read the text again and listen. Answer the questions.

1. Why do US high schools have a yearbook?
2. How did Catherine attract her schoolmates to the website?
3. Is Lunch Money real or not real, or can it be both?
4. Did the Cooks go to university, or work full-time on the website?

---

http://www.vancouver.youropinion.org

Home   About   Profiles   Match   Join!

A yearbook is a tradition of high school life in the United States. The book contains the name, picture, and signature of each student in your final year, so that you can remember who you went to school with. Fifteen-year-old New Jersey schoolgirl Catherine Cook and her brother David, 16, wanted more than this. They thought: 'We don't really know our classmates from just a picture, so why not have a yearbook online? You could learn about people's musical tastes, the movies they like, and so on.'

Catherine thought of the name (myYearbook.com), the slogan and the logo, with its two smiley faces. To advertise the site, Catherine and David wore T-shirts with the site logo on it to school and soon hundreds of their schoolmates had registered. She spent many evenings talking on the phone to programmers in India, and collecting ideas from her schoolmates. Then her older brother Geoff came up with the money to start up the website.

MyYearbook users can join in the fun by sending instant messages and 'collecting' friends. They can bond with each other by watching the same clips from films and TV programmes, and by sharing music, photos, homework and study guides. Some teens feel that they don't fit in at school, but can make friends more easily online. Chatting online helps some shy people not to feel left out.

On the site, members can also earn 'Lunch Money', a virtual currency, by completing activities on the site, or they can buy it with real cash. They can then spend their Lunch Money on virtual gifts, or donate it to charities in the myYearbook 'causes' programme. Lunch Money donations have saved 0.3km^2 of rainforest, cleaned up 1 million kg of CO_2, sent 22,000 books to Africa, and bought 20,000 kg of rice for people without enough food.

Running the website did not stop Catherine and David from completing their schoolwork successfully, and going on to university, where they still managed to put in 50 hours a week developing the site.

11 Vocabulary

✱ Making new friends

a Match the underlined expressions from the text on page 46 with the definitions a–d.

1. Users can <u>join in</u> the fun by sending instant messages.
2. They can <u>bond with</u> each other by watching clips from films.
3. Some teens feel that they don't <u>fit in</u> at school.
4. Chatting online helps some shy people not to <u>feel left out</u>.

a. feel comfortable in a group
b. be outside a group you want to be in
c. make a close connection with
d. be/feel part of

b Work with a partner. Complete the questions with an expression from Exercise 11a. Then ask and answer the questions.

1. Do you feel like you .... with all the different groups in your school?
2. Are there times when you .... because you can't do something your friends can do?
3. If you see friends playing a sport, do you .... right away or wait for them to ask you to play?
4. Do you have any good friends now that you didn't .... when you first met?

Get it right! Turn to page 67.

12 Write

a Ayşe, a student from Turkey, interviewed her classmates about their life. Read her report and put the headings in the correct place.

Conclusion   Introduction   Findings

b Work with a partner. What questions do you think Ayşe asked?

c Interview your friends and write a similar report. Use the expressions in *italic* to help you. Write 120–180 words.

---

1 ....
The aim of this report is to present information about my friends. I interviewed fifteen friends by telephone, online and in person about free time activities, music and parents.

2 ....
Free time The majority of my friends like hanging out on the beach, in the park or at the mall. *More than half* my friends go shopping every weekend. *About one in four* prefer playing basketball to football, which is *the most popular* sport. *Three out of five* go online at least five times a week, but only *about a quarter* use instant messaging. *Forty percent* play computer games every day.

Music Among my friends, *about half* usually listen to songs in English. *The other half* prefer Turkish music. *None of them* say they don't listen to any music.

Parents *Most of* my friends say that their parents allow them to stay up later than 9 pm. *Only a small number* say that their parents make them stay home to do homework at weekends.

3 ....
The most surprising aspect of the report for me is that *a large number* don't use instant messaging. I was also surprised to find out that it is *quite common* for my friends' parents to let them stay up late.

For your portfolio

UNIT 6

7 Survival

* Present passive and past passive review
* Present perfect passive
* Future passive
* Causative *have* (*have something done*)
* Vocabulary: *make* and *do*

1 Read and listen

a Look at the pictures and answer the questions.

1. In groups, discuss the possible relationship between the four photos.
2. What do you think the text is about?

b Read the text quickly to check your ideas.

Bees dying for a phone call?

1. ☐ Mobile phones are one of the most useful inventions of the last 50 years, but not everything that is said about them is good. Mobiles are frequently blamed for a number of things, from thumb injuries and headaches to house fires. One theory even blames mobile phones for the disappearance of bees!

2. ☐ The theory is that the bees' navigation systems are damaged by the radiation that is given off by mobile phones. Bees have a built-in system a bit like GPS and this helps them find their way back to their hive. But recently, thousands of bees have failed to find their way home. It is believed they are dying far from their hives.

3. ☐ The problem was first noticed by beekeepers in America and is a lot more complicated than it at first seems. The important thing about bees is that most of the crops in many countries of the world are pollinated by them. Without bees, the crops can't continue to grow. Many beekeepers in America and Europe have reported losing between 50 and 70 percent of their bees. Jim Piper, a London beekeeper, was recently asked how the problem was affecting him. 'My business has been ruined by this,' he explained. 'Twenty-nine of my forty hives are now empty.'

4. ☐ Nobody has proved that this theory is true but it's a fact that bees are disappearing in very large numbers. And we can't manage without them. Einstein said that if all our bees disappeared, man would only live for four more years! The situation needs to be evaluated by the world's best scientists. If the mobile phone theory is correct, we need to do something about it immediately – before it's too late.

c Match the titles with the paragraphs. Write the letters in the boxes. There is one title you will not use.

A It's time to act!
B Bees are losing their way
C Four years in a scientist's life
D No bees – no food
E A strange idea

d ▶ CD1 T37 Read the text again and listen. Answer the questions.

1. Why are mobile phones believed to be harmful to bees?
2. Who were the first people to notice the problem?
3. What has ruined Jim Piper's business?
4. There is no proof for the mobile phone theory, but what can we say for sure about bees?

Discussion box

1. What other problems are mobile phones causing?
2. Think of some other common animals and insects. How would the world be affected if they disappeared?

2 Grammar

★ Present passive and past passive review

a Look at the sentences from the article on page 48. Write *present simple passive* or *past simple passive* in the spaces.

*Not everything that **is said** about them is good.* _____
*The problem **was** first **noticed** by beekeepers in America.* _____

b Find more examples of the passive in the text on page 48. Then complete the rule. Use *by*, *to be* and *past participle*.

> **RULE:** We form the passive with a form of the verb _____ and the _____.
> We use the preposition _____ to say who or what does the action, but only if this is important.

c Complete the sentences with the correct form of the verbs in brackets.

1. The importance of bees __is appreciated__ (appreciate) by many farmers.
2. Hundreds of bees _____ (find) dead hundreds of metres from their hives.
3. Those hives _____ (not own) by us now; we sold them.
4. It looks as if a lot of problems _____ (cause) by mobile phones.
5. _____ any farmers _____ (interview) about the problem?
6. Quite a lot _____ (know) about how bees navigate back to the hive.
7. The theory _____ (believe) to be crazy at first.
8. _____ all crops _____ (pollinate) by bees?

3 Listen

a Grace and Mark both live in a city in the UK. There is a plan to build a new Olympic water sports centre in their city. Look at the picture. Who likes the plan? Who doesn't like it?

b ▶ CD1 T38 Listen to Grace and Mark. Mark the statements *T* (true) or *F* (false). Correct the false statements.

1. Grace forgot to bring the plans with her to the meeting. ☐
2. Grace is worried that some wild birds will lose their homes. ☐
3. Grace says that the new centre will include a play area for children. ☐
4. Grace believes there will be many new long-term jobs if the centre is built. ☐
5. Mark explains that the centre will be on unused land. ☐
6. Mark agrees the centre will create problems for the birds. ☐
7. Mark is sure the centre will be a good thing for the city. ☐

c Do you agree with Mark or Grace? Why?

UNIT 7

4 Vocabulary

★ *make* and *do*

a ▶ CD1 T38 Complete the sentences from Exercise 3 with the correct form of *make* or *do*. Then listen again and check.

1. Thanks for _making_ the effort to come to tonight's meeting.
2. That will _____ a mess of our beautiful park.
3. The Games will _____ lots of money.
4. Temporary jobs won't _____ much of a difference anyway.
5. I'm not here to _____ trouble.
6. Let's _____ our best to stop the plans right now!
7. There's no way I want to _____ fun of anything that's been said so far.
8. The centre will actually _____ some good.
9. We should all _____ the right thing.
10. You know it _____ sense.

b Put the phrases in the correct column. What other examples can you think of?

make	do
a-difference	a difference
our best	
money	
fun of (someone)	
trouble	
sense	
some good	
the effort	
a mess	
the right thing	

c Work with a partner. Take turns to make sentences about yourself and your family and friends using the phrases in Exercise 5b.

My dad always makes a mess when he cooks.

Vocabulary bank Turn to page 65.

Get it right! Turn to page 68.

5 Grammar

★ Present perfect passive

a Complete the sentences with the phrases in the box. Then complete the rule.

> have you been told
> haven't been given   have been sent

1. I _____ here by the local campaign committee.
2. You _____ a clear picture.
3. _____ about the plans for new gardens all around the centre?

> **RULE:** We form the present perfect passive with the present perfect form of the verb _____ + the _____ .

b Complete the sentences with the correct form of the verbs in brackets. Use the present perfect passive and past simple passive.

1. Town planners _were criticised_ (criticise) last week for not listening to the wishes of local people.
2. In 1908, the Olympic Games _____ (hold) here for the first time.
3. Do you know how many new hotels _____ (build) here since the 1970s?
4. A lot of money _____ (make) from the building of the new airport runway.
5. Members of the planning committee _____ (ask) some difficult questions at the meeting last week.
6. _____ many wild birds _____ (see) here since they redeveloped the area?
7. The event _____ (organise) extremely well and everything went off without any problems.
8. The centre _____ (not visit) by as many people as we expected.

✱ Future passive

c Complete the sentences with the verbs in the box.

> won't be damaged
> will be destroyed   will be lost

1. The area which is home to the swans and ducks _____ .
2. Huge play areas _____ forever.
3. As for the birds, their habitat _____ at all.

d Look at the sentences in Exercise 6a and complete the rule.

> **RULE:** We form the future passive with _____ or _____ + be + the _____ .

e Complete the text with the future passive form of the verbs in brackets.

New Bobby Moore Sports Centre

The town council has announced that a new sports centre ¹ _____ (build) over the next five years.

A competition ² _____ (hold) for the design of the sports centre, but the name of the competition winner ³ _____ (not announce) until the end of next year. The site for the new building ⁴ _____ (choose) next month. After that, the decision about which company will actually build the sports centre ⁵ _____ (make) by the town council.

6   Speak

Work with a partner and discuss the topics in the box. What things do you think will happen with each one in the future?

> space exploration   computers
> your town   language learning

A: *I think life will be found on other planets.*
B: *Perhaps computer chips will be put inside our bodies.*

7   Grammar

✱ Causative *have* (*have something done*)

a Look at the examples. In each sentence, who is the subject? Do we know who does the action?

*We need to **have the situation evaluated**.*
*We **haven't had the kitchen decorated** yet.*
***Have** you **had your computer fixed**?*

b Complete the rule with *us* and *someone*.

> **RULE:** We often use causative *have* when we arrange for _____ to do something for _____ (often as a service).

c Tom never does anything himself. Complete the sentences with the correct form of causative *have*.

1. He never washes his car himself. He always has it _____ .
2. He doesn't cut the grass in his garden. He _____ .
3. He never makes his own breakfast. He _____ .

d Make sentences that are true for you using *have* (*something*) *done* and the words from the box.

> pierce   ears   dye   hair
> shave   head   tattoo   body

1. Lots of my friends _____ .
2. None of my friends _____ .
3. My parents wouldn't allow me to _____ .
4. I would love to _____ .
5. I would hate to _____ .
6. My parents don't want me to _____ .

e Work in small groups. Share and discuss your sentences from Exercise 8d.

8   Pronunciation

✱ Stress pattern in *have something done*

▶ CD1 T39   Turn to page 62.

UNIT 7

It's not really a choice

9 Read and listen

a ▶ CD1 T40 Nick and Amy interview the man in the photo for a programme. What do you think the programme is about? Read, listen and check your ideas.

1

Duncan: Spare some change, you guys?

Amy: Yeah sure – here you are.

Duncan: Thanks, love. I appreciate it.

Nick: That's not such a good idea. You're just encouraging him.

Amy: What on earth are you talking about? I mean, he's not here because he wants to be, is he? I really don't think it's a choice.

Nick: I'm not so sure. Why don't we ask him? In fact, we could do a programme about homeless people, maybe.

Amy: Not a bad idea. Excuse me. We're from Fairbank school and we do a radio programme. Any chance we could interview you?

Duncan: Well, no, I'm not doing this because I enjoy it. I mean, it isn't fun, after all.

Amy: That's what I thought. So how come you haven't got a place to live?

Duncan: Well, before this I was living in a shared house with some other people but then I lost my job, so couldn't pay the rent. Simple as that.

Amy: Do you sleep out here?

Duncan: Sometimes. Not in winter though. Too cold. So there's a shelter I go to, a place where I can get a warm meal and a bed for the night. But I've only been in this situation for less than a year, so only one winter without a roof, you know? And last winter wasn't too bad so I didn't need the shelter much.

Amy: You survived OK?

Duncan: Yeah. That's all it is, though – surviving. All I need's a job – then I can get out of this. It's just that, when you've got no home and no money, who's going to give you a job?

Amy: So, you're stuck?

Duncan: More or less, yeah.

2

Laura: So the programme went down well.

Nick: Looks like it. And I must admit – he's a nice guy and I felt pretty sorry for him.

Amy: Well you don't need to any more. I just got some news. The principal heard the interview and he's offered him a job as assistant cleaner, here in the school.

Tom: Cool.

b Mark the sentences *T* (true) or *F* (false). Correct the false statements.

1. Amy and Nick give Duncan some money. [T]
2. Nick suggests making a programme about Duncan. [ ]
3. Duncan has been living on the street for a long time. [ ]
4. Duncan never sleeps on the street. [ ]
5. Duncan thinks that what he needs is a job. [ ]
6. The principal gave Duncan a job because he felt sorry for him. [ ]

10 Everyday English

a Find the expressions 1–6 in the story. Who says them? Match them to the meanings a–f.

1. What on earth … ?
2. Any chance … ?
3. … , after all.
4. I mean.
5. How come … ?
6. More or less, …

a … if you think about it
b used to add more information to a statement
c Is it possible …?
d very nearly; in a way
e used to add surprise or anger to a question
f What's the reason … ?

b Complete the dialogues with expressions 1–6 from Exercise 10a.

1. A: I'm going to Jake's party on Saturday. And you?
   B: I didn't know Jake was having a party. *How come* he told you but not me?
2. A: Do you like Pink?
   B: No, _____ she's OK, but I prefer dance music.
3. A: So, are you going to help Lucy?
   B: Yes, I am. She's my best friend, _____ .
4. A: Do you speak German?
   B: _____ – I mean, I can read some German but I'm not very good at speaking it.
5. A: James – _____ is that thing on your arm?
   B: It's my new tattoo. I guess you don't like it, eh?
6. A: Where's your History book, Mike?
   B: I've left it at home. _____ I could borrow yours?

Discussion box

1. Are there people in your country who ask for money in the street? If so, who are they? If not, why not?
2. If someone gives money to, for example, a homeless person like Duncan, are they helping them? Think of reasons/arguments to answer Yes or No to this question.

11 Improvisation

Work in pairs. Take two minutes to prepare a short role play. Try to use some of the expressions from Exercise 10a. Do not write the text, just agree on your ideas for a short scene. Then act it out.

Roles: Tom and Amy
Situation: At school, in the radio station studio
Basic idea: Tom promised to get an interview ready for today, but he hasn't done it.

12 Making Waves

DVD 3 Episode 2

a 1 What do you think these people are protesting about?
   2 Do you think protests like this work? Why/Why not?
   3 Have you ever been on a protest?

b Complete the news report with the words in the box

> confronted   cut down
> removed   ~~protesters~~
> playground   activist

On Thursday ¹ *protesters* led by local ² _____ Linda Crane, ³ _____ contractors sent to ⁴ _____ trees in Fairbank Fields. Other residents want the trees to be ⁵ _____ to make way for the new ⁶ _____ .

c Watch Episode 2. Does the protest work?

UNIT 7

13 Write

a Read Hilary Riley's letter to a newspaper. Why is she writing? What is she worried about?

b Read the letter again and answer the questions.

1. What useful phrase does Hilary use to state what she is worried about?
2. Underline the topic sentence in each paragraph. How does she support the idea expressed in the topic sentence?
3. What does she suggest in her conclusion?

c Imagine you are either Grace or Mark in Exercise 3. Write a letter to a newspaper about the water sports centre plan. Use Hilary's letter to help you. Write 120–150 words. Follow this plan:

- In the first paragraph, state your reason for writing.
- In the next few paragraphs, develop your ideas. Remember to use topic sentences.
- To conclude, state what you think should happen / should be done.

Dear Sir

I am writing to express my concern about the plans to build a motorway near our village.

Haldersham is one of the loveliest villages in England. It is peaceful and quiet, and it is situated in a very attractive valley. There are also several beautiful countryside walks in the surroundings.

Most of the people who live in Haldersham have moved here from other places, often from London. They have bought houses here to live in a place far away from the noise and the stress of the big city. They paid a lot of money for their houses, but they knew they would get a high quality of life for it.

If the planned motorway is built, life in Haldersham will change dramatically. There will be a lot of noise, and nobody will want to go on the walks. House prices will certainly go down, because nobody will want to buy houses in a place close to a motorway. Haldersham will become an ugly place.

I don't think any of the residents of our beautiful village want that. So, let's all tell the politicians who support the motorway plans what we think about them!

Yours faithfully

Hilary Riley

Hilary Riley

---

14 Last but not least: more speaking

a Read the proposals. Imagine that they are about your town. How would you feel about each one? Give each statement a number from 1 (very angry) to 4 (not at all angry).

- ☐ The town council wants to turn the local park into a large shopping centre.
- ☐ The police want to ban anyone under 18 from being in town after 10 pm.
- ☐ The town council has refused permission for a free music festival.
- ☐ The town council want to sell the town football team to a billionaire who will increase ticket prices by 50%.

b Compare ideas with a partner. Discuss why (or why not) these proposals would worry you.

c Work in groups. Choose one of the proposals that you all feel strongly about and decide on a campaign against it. Think about:

- ways you can draw attention to the issue.
- action you can take to try and stop the proposal.
- people you could ask to help you with your campaign.
- a possible compromise.

Check your progress

1 Grammar

a Complete the sentences. Use modal verbs of permission, obligation and prohibition.

1. My teacher caught me sleeping in class and I _had to_ stay behind after class.
2. It's a really big secret, OK? You _____ tell anyone.
3. I _____ come to your party. Mum says I'm not allowed to.
4. _____ you _____ wear a uniform to school?
5. I'm not completely stupid, you know. You _____ explain *everything* to me!

[4]

b Complete the paragraph. Use the correct form of the past simple passive or the present perfect passive.

The radio _was invented_ (invent) at the beginning of the 20th century. In the First World War, radios [1]_____ (use) to communicate with soldiers. Since the 1960s, many radio signals [2]_____ (send) into outer space. So far, no answers [3]_____ (receive) from other planets. It's possible that the signals have arrived on other planets, but the messages [4]_____ (not understand).

[4]

c Complete the paragraph. Use the correct future passive form of the verbs in the box.

send   examine   not answer
~~explore~~   bring   find

The planet Mars [1]_will be explored_ during the next few years. Special robot vehicles [2]_____ to investigate the planet's surface. It is possible that rocks and dust from Mars [3]_____ back to Earth when the vehicles return. These rocks [4]_____ to find out if it is possible to live on Mars. The questions about the Red Planet [5]_____ for a very long time.

[4]

e Rewrite the sentences, using the correct form of causative *have*.

1. Someone repaired my bike for me last week. _I had my bike repaired last week._
2. Someone cuts Mr Hart's hair every month. Mr Hart _____.
3. Someone has repaired my laptop. I _____.
4. Someone is going to install cable TV for us tomorrow. We're _____.

[3]

2 Vocabulary

a Complete the sentences with the extreme adjective.

1. I'm not just hungry, I'm _starving_.
2. It's not small, it's _____.
3. Cold? I'm absolutely _____.
4. It was more than interesting – it was _____.
5. That's funny. Actually, it's _____.
6. Are you tired too? I'm absolutely _____.

[5]

b (Circle) the correct verb.

1. It (makes) / *does* sense to go to bed early the night before an exam.
2. Yesterday I *did* / *made* a big effort and got up early!
3. You failed the exam? Don't worry, I'm sure you *did* / *made* your best.
4. He wants to *do* / *make* a lot of money.
5. Drink this. It'll *make* / *do* you good.
6. It really *makes* / *does* a big difference when you type more slowly.

[5]

How did you do?

Check your score.

Total score	😊 Very good	😐 OK	☹ Not very good
[25]			
Grammar	12 – 15	7 – 11	less than 7
Vocabulary	8 – 10	5 – 7	less than 5

8 Good and evil

* Gerunds and infinitives
* Vocabulary: noun suffixes

1 Read and listen

a Read the texts quickly and match them with the pictures. Which story would you read first?

1 JANE EYRE
by Charlotte Brontë

Jane, an orphan, is sent to live with her kind uncle, but he soon dies. Jane can't stand living with her evil aunt. At the age of ten, she is sent away to a boarding school with a cruel headmaster. Later she becomes a teacher at the school but decides to leave and becomes a governess at Thornfield Manor, a big house in the countryside. Here she meets the moody but fascinating Mr. Rochester – a man with a dark secret that will bring them close to disaster.

2 DRACULA
by Bram Stoker

Lawyer Jonathan Harker travels to Count Dracula's castle in Eastern Europe to take the Count some papers to sign for a house he wants to buy in England. The Count is charming at first, but as time goes by, Jonathan discovers some strange things. Why does the Count avoid seeing Jonathan during the day, and why does he have no reflection in the mirror? How can he crawl down the wall like an animal? The Count leaves Jonathan as a prisoner and disappears. In England, Jonathan's fiancée is followed by a large, mysterious 'wolf'. The wolf has jumped off a ship from Eastern Europe.

3 LORD OF THE FLIES
by William Golding

A group of schoolboys survive when their plane crashes on an island. Ralph becomes the leader, and the boys work together to build a shelter and gather food and water to stay alive. Jack takes charge of a group hunting animals. Some of the younger children say they have been chased by a strange beast. Jack promises to kill the beast, but Ralph wants to concentrate on getting off the island. Some boys go with Jack, and the others stay with Ralph. Here begins a classic battle of good versus evil.

4 THE HOBBIT
by J.R.R. Tolkien

Bilbo Baggins enjoys living an ordinary life. This changes forever when Gandalf the Wizard persuades him to join a band of dwarves. They go on an adventure to get back a lost kingdom and treasure. Bilbo meets many characters, both good and evil, along the way. Gollum, a nasty creature, traps Bilbo in a cave, but offers to free him if he can solve a riddle. Bilbo manages to escape after he finds Gollum's magic ring. This makes him invisible.

b ▶ CD2 T2 Read the texts again and listen. Answer the questions. There may be more than one possible answer.

1. Who:
    a. becomes an animal hunter?
    b. goes on a treasure hunt?
    c. is a prisoner?
    d. escapes?

2. What do you think:
    a. Mr. Rochester's secret is?
    b. the mysterious 'wolf' is?
    c. happens to Jack and Ralph?
    d. happens to Gollum's ring?

Discussion box

Choose one of the stories and make suggestions about what you think happens next.

2 Grammar

✱ Gerunds and infinitives

a Look at the sentences from the texts on page 56. The missing verbs are followed by a verb in the *-ing* form (a gerund). Complete the sentences with the correct forms of the verbs.

1. Jane _____ living with her evil aunt.
2. Why does the Count _____ seeing Jonathan during the day?
3. Bilbo Baggins _____ living an ordinary life.

b The missing verbs in these sentences are followed by *to* + infinitive. Complete the sentences with the correct forms of the verbs. Use the texts on page 56 to help you.

1. Jane _____ to leave the school.
2. Count Dracula _____ to buy a house in England.
3. Jack _____ to kill the beast.
4. Gollum _____ to free Bilbo if he can solve a riddle.

c Read the rule and (circle) the correct words.

> **RULE:** The verbs *enjoy*, *(don't) mind*, *(can't) stand*, *imagine*, *feel like*, *suggest*, *practise*, *miss* and *avoid* are all followed by *to* + infinitive / a gerund.
> The verbs *hope*, *promise*, *learn*, *expect*, *decide*, *afford*, *offer*, *choose* and *want* are followed by *to* + infinitive / a gerund.

d Complete the text with the correct form of the verbs in the box.

> ~~move~~   cross   go   hear   sing   see   have   shout

A few years ago, we lived in a house by the sea but then my parents suggested ¹ *moving* to another house, in the town centre. So we moved.

It was OK living in the city – I enjoyed ² _____ to the shopping centre near my new home, for example, and I didn't mind ³ _____ other houses from my window – but I couldn't stand ⁴ _____ all those busy streets! Sometimes I felt like ⁵ _____ at the drivers of all those cars!

I always loved living by the sea, and I missed ⁶ _____ the sound of the waves outside our old house. Sometimes I imagined ⁷ _____ a house of my own, on the beach, where I could live alone and practise ⁸ _____ without annoying anyone!

e Complete the sentences with the correct form of a verb from box A and a verb from box B. Make any necessary changes to the verb tenses.

> **A**
> hope   offer
> ~~choose~~   learn
> (not) expect
> afford   decide
> promise

> **B**
> do   call
> live   help
> lend   ~~stay~~
> play   buy

1. I can't believe you *chose to stay* at home rather than come to the party with us.
2. After a lot of thought, I _____ you my MP3 player – but just for one night!
3. When I'm older, I _____ in New York or San Francisco.
4. My brother _____ me with my homework last night.
5. My sister _____ tennis – and she's making good progress!
6. I'm amazed at my exam results – I _____ so well!
7. I can't _____ any computer games this month. I've got no money left!
8. You _____ me last night, but you didn't! I left my phone on all night waiting for you.

3 Speak

a Work with a partner. How well do you know them? Take a guess and complete the sentences for them.

For your next birthday, you hope …

At the weekend, you really enjoy …

For your next holiday, you want …

When you can, you avoid …

If you move away from this town, you will miss …

b Compare ideas with your partner.

UNIT 8

4 Speak and listen

a Do you or your friends play any of the games in the pictures? How much time do you spend each week playing computer games?

b Use the words in the box to describe your favourite game.

> puzzles to solve   realistic graphics   sound
> strategy   characters   manoeuvres   story

c ▶ CD2 T3 Listen to Sarah talking about her favourite game. Answer the questions.

1. Is her favourite game new or old?
2. What school subject is she studying because of the game?
3. What does the main character (the Prince) need to do to win the game?

d ▶ CD2 T3 Listen again and complete the summary.

> 1 The game first appeared in ^{1}_____ , and has since been made into a ^{2}_____ . Sarah borrowed the game from her ^{3}_____ . The game and the film have the same ^{4}_____ , but the story is ^{5}_____ . For example, in the game, the Prince hasn't got a ^{6}_____ . Sarah especially likes the background ^{7}_____ , the interesting ^{8}_____ , the amazing ^{9}_____ , and the way you can control ^{10}_____ .

5 Vocabulary

✱ **Noun suffixes**

a (Circle) the incorrect word in these sentences from Exercise 4. Which one is the noun?

1. The story is a bit *different / difference* from the film.
2. I wanted to see what the *different / difference* was.

Vocabulary bank Turn to page 65.

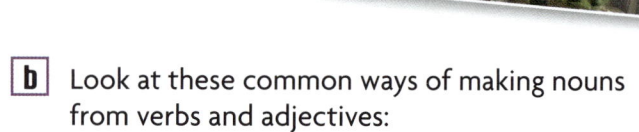

b Look at these common ways of making nouns from verbs and adjectives:

> -ation   -ion   -ness   -ment   -ence   -ity

imagine → imagination   enjoy → enjoyment
protect → protection   different → difference
kind → kindness   possible → possibility

Make nouns from these verbs and adjectives.

1. agree
2. prefer
3. react
4. entertain
5. prepare
6. popular
7. relax
8. happy

c Complete the sentences with nouns from Exercise 5b.

1. Listening to music, for me, is the best kind of _relaxation_ that there is.
2. Madonna is still a very successful singer. Her _____ is enormous.
3. If you haven't got much time, make a fruit salad. It doesn't need a lot of _____ .
4. My father wanted to buy that car, but he couldn't come to an _____ about the price with the owner.
5. I was surprised by her _____ when I told her about the plan.
6. What did people do for _____ before TV?

UNIT 8

6 Pronunciation
★ Word stress

▶ CD2 T4 Turn to page 62.

7 Grammar
★ Verbs with gerunds or infinitives

a Look at the sentences from Exercise 4, then read and complete the rule with *different* or *no difference*.

I **love to look** at the amazing background graphics.
I **love solving** the interesting puzzles.
I **remember playing** it when it came out in 2003.
You have to **remember to jump** at the right time.

> **RULE:** The verb *love* can be followed by a gerund or infinitive, with _____ in meaning. The verbs *like, hate, prefer, begin* and *start* follow the same rule as *love*.
>
> The verb *remember* can also be followed by a gerund or infinitive – but the meaning is _____ .
>
> *I remember paying* (= I paid and now I remember that.)
>
> *You have to remember to jump* (= you have to remember and then you jump.)
>
> The verb *stop* also changes its meaning, e.g. *I stopped eating chocolate six months ago.* (= I ate chocolate until six months ago but then I stopped.)
>
> *I was in town shopping, and I stopped to eat a sandwich.* (= I stopped and then I ate a sandwich.)

b Circle the correct words in the sentences.

1. I remember *to meet / meeting* Ellie at a party a few months ago.
2. Don't worry – I'll remember *to give / giving* you the book back.
3. Please stop *to make / making* so much noise! I want to go to sleep!
4. It was really hot in the car, so we stopped *to buy / buying* some ice creams.

Get it right! Turn to page 68.

c Complete the sentences with the correct form of the verbs in brackets. There may be more than one correct answer.

1. I love ____*playing*____ (play) games on my PC when I get home from school.
2. He's a nice guy, but he never stops _____ (talk) about football!
3. Did you remember _____ (email) your sister?
4. Have you started _____ (read) your new *Twilight* book yet?
5. Do you prefer _____ (watch) horror films or comedies?
6. I don't remember _____ (rent) this DVD before. Are you sure we've seen it?
7. I really hate _____ (do) homework when it's sunny outside.
8. I'm really hungry. Can we stop _____ (get) a sandwich?

> **LOOK!**
> *would like / would love / would hate / would prefer* are always followed by the infinitive.
> *I would like to go to the cinema.*

8 Speak

a Work with a partner. Student B: Turn to page 71.

Student A: On a piece of paper, write something:

- you must remember to do next week.
- you like doing when you want to relax.
- you started doing a couple of years ago.
- you hate doing.

walking to school

b Look at what your partner wrote, and try to guess why. Have a conversation using verbs from Exercise 7 to help you.

A: 'Walking to school.' Is that something you hate doing?
B: No, it's something I started doing a couple of years ago. I stopped cycling and started walking to school.

UNIT 8

Fiction in mind

9 Read and listen

a These scientists all do something that causes problems. Do you know any of them? What can you say about them?

Frankenstein   Dr Jekyll and Mr Hyde   The Hulk

The Water of Wanting
a short story from Tasty Tales, *by Frank Brennan*

The story so far:
Jean Pascal is a research scientist for a big company that makes chemicals to put in foods – additives. He has made a liquid that he calls WOW – 'water of wanting' – that you can add to drinks or food. Jean is in the office of his manager, Charles, to tell him about the liquid.

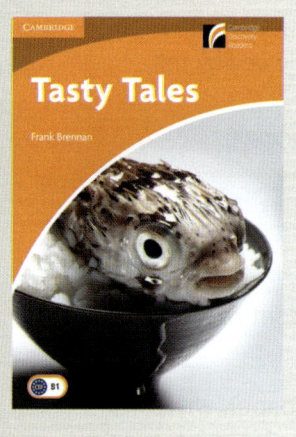

Jean looked a little uncomfortable, but he lifted up his eyes and looked into Charles's worried face and began, 'WOW is a liquid which you can't see and you can't smell, a liquid which is – in itself – completely harmless.' Jean could see Charles nodding his head and smiling widely. 'In carefully measured amounts, it can make a person prefer one kind of drink over another –'

'Hey, Jean!' Charles cried out. 'That's brilliant! Just what we wanted!'

'I haven't finished, Charles ...'

Charles apologised, still nodding his head, and Jean continued.

'However, if these amounts are exceeded ... I mean, if we put too much WOW into a product, people will want the product so much that it becomes really dangerous. The person will eat or drink until they are dead. The person has to have the product – they have no choice.'

For a moment, Charles stopped smiling. 'So what you're saying is: if we add too much WOW to something, it's going to make it dangerous?'

'That's right.'

'But, if the amounts are right, we can use WOW safely, right?'

'Well, yes, but – '

'No problem then!' Charles laughed. 'I'm sure it'll be perfectly OK, Jean. I'll make sure everyone understands.'

'No, Charles,' Jean said, more impatiently this time. 'Let me explain. I've been doing some thinking about this lately – '

'You certainly have, Mr Clever!' said Charles. '[...] We're going to make millions on this one, Jean. Millions!'

'Charles!' Jean raised his voice. 'Let me explain more clearly. WOW is dangerous! If it's used in the wrong amounts, it can make people crazy ... crazy with a need for ... for anything they eat or drink. And then they won't want to eat or drink anything else at all! [...]

'Well,' Charles replied, more calmly now, 'I see your point now, Jean. We have to be careful with these things.'

'At first,' Jean said, 'I was excited by the idea of helping people to eat good food. There are too many fat people these days; I wanted to help with the problems.'

'Oh, yes!' Charles said. 'Of course!'

'Yes, well', Jean replied [...], 'I realise now that I was playing with fire. It'll be better if the research is put away and forgotten about. It's too dangerous and just too ... too *wrong*. You can see that now, can't you, Charles?'

b ▶ CD2 T5 Read the extract and listen. Mark the sentences *T* (true), *F* (false) or *NI* (no information).

1. The right amount of *WOW* in a drink makes people want more of the drink. ☐
2. *WOW* could be used to make people buy more of anything, not just food and drink. ☐
3. Jean says that *WOW* can be dangerous if too much of it is used. ☐
4. Too much *WOW* in a product will make people want to eat or drink only that product. ☐
5. Charles says he's going to make millions of bottles of *WOW*. ☐
6. Jean thought that *WOW* could be used to help people with problems. ☐
7. Charles now thinks that using *WOW* would be wrong. ☐

c Here are three things that could happen next in the story. Which one do you think is correct?

1. Charles kills Jean and starts to sell *WOW*, and he makes a lot of money.
2. Charles decides to make and sell *WOW* but doesn't tell Jean.
3. Charles decides that *WOW* is too dangerous to sell, so Jean starts selling it secretly.

Discussion box
1. What do you think Jean should do?
2. Do you think it's possible for something like *WOW* to be invented? Why (not)?

10 Write

a Read the text about eating fast food and answer the questions.

1. Which paragraph talks about the advantages of eating fast food? What are the advantages?
2. Which paragraph talks about the disadvantages of fast food? What are they?
3. Does the writer think that eating fast food is a good or bad idea?

b Which of the underlined words in the text are used to introduce:

1. the conclusion?
2. another point supporting the previous ideas?
3. the opposite side of an argument?
4. the consequence of an action?

What are the advantages and disadvantages of eating fast food?

Many people do not have time to eat home-cooked food. <u>Because of</u> our non-stop modern lifestyle, fast food is popular almost everywhere. In most cities, it is not difficult to find hamburgers, pizza, or fried chicken.

Eating fast food helps working people and students to get back to work as quickly as possible. <u>In addition</u>, many love the look, smell and taste of it. Perhaps the greatest advantage is the price. It is often cheaper than other kinds of restaurant food.

<u>On the other hand</u>, many people feel that fast food is unhealthy because it contains a lot of artificial ingredients. In fact, some even think that it is addictive because of these ingredients, and also because fast food companies advertise so much. They blame fast food for making people much fatter than before.

<u>To sum up</u>, there are both advantages and disadvantages to fast food. I believe that it can be a good thing, as long as people do not eat it too often, eat plenty of fruit and vegetables, and also do plenty of exercise to keep in shape.

c Write about one of the following topics. Use the text on fast food to help you. Remember to use topic sentences. Write 120–180 words.

What are the advantages and disadvantages of:
- using the internet?
- playing computer games?
- mobile phones?

For your portfolio

Pronunciation

🔴 Unit 2 Sentence stress

▶ CD1 T13 Listen to the questions and mark the stressed words. Then listen, check and repeat.

1 Can you tell us another secret?
2 Was it really that easy?
3 So how can I use it?
4 What on earth is that?
5 What can I do to communicate better?

🔴 Unit 3 Linking sounds

▶ CD1 T18 Listen to the sentences. How do you pronounce the underlined parts? Then listen, check and repeat.

1 I always <u>stick up</u> for my friends.
2 I can't lie, but I don't want <u>to tell on</u> a friend.
3 Why should I <u>get into</u> trouble for something I haven't done?
4 I'm <u>surprised anyone gets on</u> with you.

🔵 Unit 4 /ɔː/ short

a ▶ CD1 T21 Listen and repeat.

1 more   2 four   3 before   4 saw   5 short

b ▶ CD1 T22 Underline the syllables with the /ɔː/ sound. Then listen, check and repeat.

1 I saw the ball, and I caught it.
2 We can't play tennis here – the court's too short!
3 We ought to buy four more.
4 But we bought forty before!

🔵 Unit 5 Prepositions

▶ CD1 T30 Listen to the sentences. Circle the prepositions where they are weak. Underline the prepositions where they are strong. Then listen, check and repeat.

1 I'm revising for my exams.
2 What are you looking for?
3 I can't stand talking to him.
4 Who's John talking to?
5 Who are you looking at?
6 I think he's at work.

🟢 Unit 6 /aʊ/ all<u>ow</u>ed

a ▶ CD1 T33 Listen and repeat.

1 cow   2 house   3 round   4 town
5 shower   6 allowed

b ▶ CD1 T34 Underline the syllables with the /aʊ/ sound. Then listen, check and repeat.

1 How are you now?
2 I'm allowed to have a mouse in the house.
3 You aren't allowed to sing loudly in the shower.

🟢 Unit 7 Stress pattern in *have something done*

▶ CD1 T39 Listen and mark the words that are stressed. Then listen, check and repeat.

1 Have you had your hair cut?
2 Dad's going to have a phone installed.
3 They had the road closed.
4 They had the people removed.
5 Have you had your camera fixed?
6 He's having a garage built.

🟣 Unit 8 Word stress

▶ CD2 T4 Underline the syllables you think are stressed. Then listen, check and repeat.

1 imagine   2 imagination
3 refer   4 reference
5 popular   6 popularity
7 possible   8 possibility
9 relax   10 relaxation

62 PRONUNCIATION

Vocabulary bank

Unit 2 Collocations with *talk* and *speak*

talk

1. **to talk back** = to reply in a rude way to someone you should be polite to
   Our teacher was really angry with Alex because he **talked back** to her.

2. **to talk nonsense** = to say things which are silly and not true
   You can't have a discussion with Paul – he **talks nonsense** all the time!

3. **to talk** + noun = to talk about a particular subject
   When Gary and Jane get together, they just **talk clothes** all the time.

4. **to talk shop** = to talk about your job with the people you work with, even when you are not at work
   My mum and dad work in the same bank, and in the evening they **talk shop** all the time!

5. **talk about** + adjective = an expression used to emphasise the adjective you are using
   Did you see the match last night? **Talk about exciting!** It was fantastic!

speak

6. **to speak up** = to speak more loudly, so that other people can hear
   Sorry, but we can't hear you at the back of the room. Can you **speak up**, please?

7. **to speak too soon** = to say something which you quickly see is not true
   I'm sure John isn't coming to the party. Oh, I **spoke too soon**. Look! He's just arrived.

8. **to speak** + possessive adjective + **mind** = to say strongly and directly what you think about something
   Look, Tom, I'm going to **speak my mind**, OK? I think you were really rude to Mandy and you should say sorry.

9. **not be on speaking terms** [with someone] = to not speak to someone because you have had an argument
   James and Allie had an argument last night – now they're **not on speaking terms**.

10. **can't speak a word of** + language = can't say anything in a foreign language
    I've been to Greece lots of times – but I **can't speak a word of Greek**!

Unit 3 Friends

1. **an old friend** = someone who has been a friend for a long time
   Jim and I are **old friends** – I've known him since I was four!

2. **a close friend** = a friend who you know very well and really trust
   Belinda knows all my secrets! She's a really **close friend**.

3. **to make friends** = to start a friendship
   Joanna's very sociable and finds it very easy **to make** new **friends**.

4. **That's what friends are for** = you can say this to a friend who thanks you for doing something special for them
   'Thanks so much, Jenny – you really helped me.' 'No problem, Mike – **that's what friends are for**.'

5. **to hit it off** [with someone] = to like someone and become friendly immediately
   Alex and I **hit it off** when we met and now we're really good friends.

6. **a mate** [informal, British English] = a friend
   We've been **mates** for years now. We met at primary school.

7. **an ally** = a country or person who helps you in a war or time of difficulty
   The USA, France and Britain were **allies** in the Second World War.

8. **an acquaintance** = someone you know but who is not really a friend
   He's not really my dad's friend, he's just **an acquaintance** from work.

VOCABULARY BANK 63

Unit 5 Verb + preposition combinations: *with/for/about*

1. I **had fun with** my mates yesterday – we watched some DVDs and played some computer games.
2. I like to **chat with** my friends after school – we just talk about little things, nothing important, but it's nice!
3. My parents don't like some of the people I **go round with**.
4. That yellow shirt's very nice, but it doesn't really **go with** green trousers.
5. Everything on the menu looks great, but I think I'll **go for** the spaghetti.
6. We can't play cricket if it's raining, so we're **praying for** good weather for tomorrow's match.
7. My sister's just graduated from university and now she's **applying for** jobs with lots of different companies.
8. My dog's really ill. The vet says we can only **hope for** the best, but we think he may not live very long.
9. I don't like being with John. After the first five minutes together, we don't have anything to **talk about**.
10. I just don't think it's funny. There's nothing to **laugh about**!
11. He used to **dream about** being rich – and then he won the lottery and now he is rich!
12. Look, I think one thing and you don't agree – but we don't need to **argue about** it, do we?

Unit 6 Extreme adjectives

1. The food at that restaurant is really **delicious** = it tastes very good
2. I couldn't eat the food – it was **disgusting** = it tasted very bad 
3. We watched a comedy programme last night – it was **hilarious**! = it was very funny 
4. We went to a rock concert and the music was **deafening**! = it was very loud 
5. We watched a **fascinating** programme about whales = it was very interesting 
6. We were **delighted** when we heard your good news = we were very happy 
7. There was a **terrible** accident last week – three people were killed = it was very bad 
8. I went bungee jumping yesterday – I was **terrified**! = I was very frightened 
9. At the end of the race, I was **thrilled** because I won! = very excited 

VOCABULARY BANK

Unit 7 Expressions with *make*

1. **to make a request** = to ask (for) something
   John, can I **make a request**? Can we start the meeting at 10am, not 9am?

2. **to make an offer** = to say that you will do something or that you will pay a price
   I didn't really want to sell my bike, but Graham **made** me **an offer** of €250, so I took it.

3. **to make a start** = to begin (work)
   There's a lot of work to do today, so we should **make a start** now, I think.

4. **to make a living** = to earn money that you use to buy food, clothes, etc.
   She doesn't like her job at all – it's just a way for her to **make a living**.

5. **to make time** = to find space in a day to do something
   I'm really busy tomorrow, but I'll try to **make time** to phone you, OK?

6. **to make sure** = to take action to be certain that something happens, is true, etc.
   I think I locked the door – but I'll go back to the house to **make sure**.

7. **to make room (for)** = to leave space for something, so that it can go in
   Our new television is really big! We had to take the sofa out of the living room to **make room** for it!

8. **to make way (for)** = to be replaced by something, especially because it is better, cheaper, easier, etc.
   They knocked down six shops in that street to **make way** for a new supermarket.

Unit 8 Noun suffixes: *-ity/-ment/-ness/-ion/-ation*

1. **probability** [adjective: *probable*]
   James loves films, so in all **probability** he's at the cinema right now.

2. **creativity** [adjective: *creative*]
   Writers need a lot of **creativity** – they have to imagine people and places, and tell a good story.

3. **amusement** [verb: *amuse*]
   I came last in the race, to my brother's **amusement**. He thought it was really funny.

4. **treatment** [verb: *treat*]
   She gets special **treatment** from the teachers because she's so good at sport – it's not fair!

5. **punishment** [verb: *punish*]
   I came home really late last night, so my parents say I can't go out for a week as a **punishment**.

6. **advertisement** [verb: *advertise*]
   I bought this camera because I saw an **advertisement** for it in a magazine.

7. **madness** [adjective: *mad*]
   It's raining and you're going out for a walk? That's complete **madness**!

8. **blindness** [adjective: *blind*]
   Some people have problems with their eyes – and if they don't get medical help, it can result in **blindness**.

9. **action** [verb: *act*]
   We can't just sit here and talk about the problem – we need to take **action**!

10. **suggestion** [verb: *suggest*]
    So, what are we going to do? Has anyone got a **suggestion**?

11. **expectations** [verb: *expect*]
    People have very high **expectations** of the new president – let's hope she does a good job!

12. **invitation** [verb: *invite*]
    Sorry, you can't come in – it's **invitation** only and you're not on the guest list.

VOCABULARY BANK

Get it right!

Unit 2

> **say and tell**
>
> *tell* is usually followed by a person (the listener):
> He **told me** about his family. **Not** He told about his family.
>
> *say* is not followed by a person:
> My mum **said that** I can go. **Not** My mum said me that I can go.
>
> If we want to add a listener, we can sometimes use *say something to someone*:
> Did she **say** anything **to you** about it?

Tick (✓) the correct sentence.

1. a I'd like to tell you about where I live. ✓
   b I'd like to tell about where I live.
2. a We told to the police everything.
   b We told the police everything.
3. a What did he say you then?
   b What did he say then?
4. a Most people said the film was terrible.
   b Most people told the film was terrible.
5. a They didn't say their parents about it.
   b They didn't tell their parents about it.
6. a I had nothing to say him.
   b I had nothing to say to him.

Unit 3

> **Spelling – regular verb endings**
>
> For most regular verbs in English, you add *-ing* to form the present participle and *-ed* to form the past simple and past participle:
> work – working – worked
>
> For verbs ending vowel + consonant (*stop, chat*), you double the final consonant:
> stop – stopping – stopped
>
> But for verbs ending in two vowels + consonant (*wait, need*), you don't double the final letter:
> wait – waiting – waited
>
> For verbs ending in *-y* (*study, try*), you drop the *-y* and add *-ied* to form the past simple and past participle:
> study – studying – studied
>
> But for verbs ending *-ay, -ey, -oy, -uy* (*play, enjoy*), you just add the regular endings:
> play – playing – played
>
> There are also many irregular verbs in English:
> She **chose** a seat by the window. **Not** She choosed a seat by the window.
> Anya **left** the party early. **Not** Anya leaved the party early.
>
> Use the table on page 72 to help you learn these.

a Underline the spelling errors and correct them.

1. They spend too much time <u>plaing</u> computer games.   *playing*
2. Harris tryed to escape, but he didn't stand a chance.
3. I think they really enjoyed playing with the children.
4. Some of the children cryed or screamed.
5. They staied in Ecuador for two months and studied the animals.

b Write the correct form of the verbs in brackets.

1. I ___*bought*___ (buy) these trousers at the market, they only _____ (cost) €15.
2. Which book have you _____ (choose) to read next?
3. It's called *Animal Farm*. Have you _____ (read) it?
4. Suddenly he _____ (hear) a noise outside.
5. Have the police _____ (catch) the murderer yet?
6. The cyclist _____ (fall) over and _____ (hurt) her arm.

Unit 4

work or job?

These words are both used to talk about things we do to earn money, but they're used in different ways:
I decided to **find a job**.
I applied for a job. Not *I applied for a work.*
He's **got a job** in a museum.
They **go to work** by bus.
I **start/finish work** at 8 o'clock.

Remember, *job* is a countable noun and *work* is uncountable:
I'm looking for **a part-time job** or I'm looking for part-time **work**.
It wasn't **a very exciting job** or It wasn't very exciting **work**.

Complete the text with *job* or *work*.

Every summer, in the school holidays I look for a _job_ to earn some money. Last year, I got a ¹_____ on a farm, picking strawberries. We had to start ²_____ at 7 in the morning. It was really hard ³_____ bending down all day. The only good thing was we finished ⁴_____ at 2pm. This year, I've applied for a summer ⁵_____ in a hotel. I'd like a career in tourism, so it'll be good ⁶_____ experience.

Unit 5

Verbs with prepositions

Some verbs are usually followed by a preposition:
about
What do you **know about** computers?
Young people should **learn about** the past.
We **told** him **about** our problem.
for
I've **applied for** a new job.
He **asked for** more information.
I'll **pay for** the tickets.
with
She never **agrees with** her parents.
Can you **help** me **with** this exercise?

Complete the dialogue with *about*, *for* or *with*.

Jo: I'm really worried _about_ this project I've got to do. Can you help me ¹_____ it?
Sam: Yeah, sure. What's the topic?
Jo: We've got to write ²_____ the effects of information technology in the workplace.
Sam: Oh, I don't really know much ³_____ IT. Why don't you ask your Mum ⁴_____ some ideas. She works ⁵_____ a computer company, doesn't she?
Jo: Yeah, of course. Great idea I'll talk to her ⁶_____ it this evening. Hey Sam, thanks ⁷_____ your help!

Unit 6

Making new friends

We talk about *meeting people*, but *making friends*:
I **met** lots of interesting **people**.
I'm sure you'll **make** new **friends**. Not *I'm sure you'll meet/find new friends.*

If you *know* someone, they are already your friend:
I've **known** Sonya for about four years.

But you *get to know* a new friend:
I **got to know** a lot of new people. Not *I knew I lot of new people.*

Underline the correct verb or verb phrase.

1 I've <u>known</u> / met Sven since we were little kids.
2 At the camp, they *knew / met* people from lots of different countries.
3 He'll soon *make / do* friends with some of his new classmates.
4 On holiday, we *knew / got to know* a couple of lads from Holland.
5 When you move to a new area, it can be difficult to *meet / make* friends.
6 Joining a club is a good way to *meet / know* new people.

GET IT RIGHT! 67

Unit 7

make or do?

The common verbs *make* and *do* are often used with particular nouns:

She **made** no **effort** to escape. **Not** She did no effort to escape.

I'll **make** all the **arrangements**. **Not** I'll do all the arrangements.

I'll **do my best** to help. **Not** I'll make my best to help.

We **did** a lot of **sightseeing**. **Not** We made a lot of sightseeing.

Use the table on page 50 and the Vocabulary bank on page 65 to help you learn some common verb and noun pairs.

Complete the sentences with the correct form of *make* or *do*.

1 Most artists don't ......*make*...... much money.
2 I .... a lot of phone calls to my family while I was away.
3 Have you .... your homework yet?
4 Do you .... a lot of sport?
5 I called the doctor to .... an appointment.
6 I think they need to .... some changes.
7 Sometimes, people .... fun of his voice.
8 Are we going to .... the same thing next week?

Unit 8

Verbs with gerunds and infinitives

Some verbs are followed by a gerund:
Try to **avoid travelling** at peak times.
Not Try to avoid to travel at peak times.

Some verbs are followed by *to* + infinitive:
Children **learn to read** at primary school.
Not Children learn reading at primary school.

Remember! If there's more than one following verb, they are both in the same form:
I **enjoy walking** in the countryside and **taking** photos.

You don't need to repeat *to* before a second infinitive:
They **decided to go** home and **have** something to eat.

Complete the text with the correct form of the verbs in brackets.

Last weekend, Max and I decided ......*to go*...... (go) to the cinema. Max wanted [1].................... (see) the new James Bond film, but there was a huge queue and I didn't feel like [2].................... (stand) around and [3].................... (wait) in a queue for ages. So I suggested [4].................... (go) for something less popular and in the end, we decided [5].................... (watch) a little independent movie instead. I expected it [6].................... (be) a bit rubbish, but it was actually the best film I've seen all year!

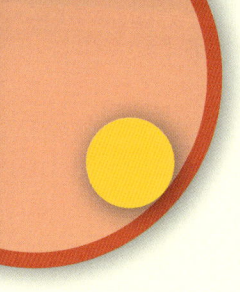

Project 1

Class research: how we communicate

1 Brainstorm and prepare

a Work in small groups. How much time a day do you spend talking? How much time do you spend using a mobile phone? You are each going to take part in an experiment about communication by keeping a diary of exactly how you communicate during one day. Make a group list of all the ways you communicate.

> talking face-to-face
> writing notes on paper
> using face/body gestures

b Each person in the group should copy the list into a table, for example:

How	Number of times	How long for
talking face-to-face	IIII	2mins/30secs/10secs/4mins
writing notes on paper	I	30secs
using face/body gestures	III	2secs/3secs/3secs

c Choose a day to do your research, and keep your list with you! Record how many times you use each method of communication, and how long you use each method for. Add new things to the table if necessary. Promise to be as accurate as you can!

2 Collect results

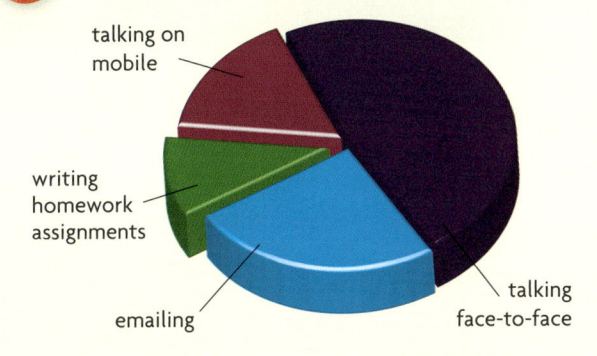

(Pie chart: talking on mobile, writing homework assignments, emailing, talking face-to-face)

a Work in your group again. Total the number of times you used each method of communication, and the total time spent on each one. Are there any big differences in your group?

b Decide on different ways to present your group's results to the class. For example, one person could present a pie chart, one person a graph, and another could describe the most interesting part of the research.

3 Share and discuss

Present your results to the class. What do the results mean? What could be wrong with the research? Does anything surprise you? Will you change the way you communicate?

> I'm surprised I don't talk that much.

> I text way too much!

> Gestures only took ten seconds, but I said a lot with them!

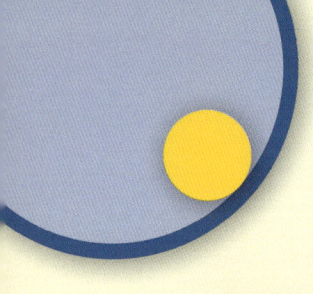

Project 2

Plan a TV show

1 Start thinking

In small groups, make a list of TV programmes which do not use actors. Use the following categories:

> ordinary people at home or work
> quizzes and games
> dangerous situations or competitions
> voting for the best singer/dancer/model, etc.
> changing something about your life (clothes/appearance/house, etc.)

2 Plan the show

Your group is going to think of a new reality TV programme. It should be different in some way from programmes already on TV. Make a detailed plan for the show. Consider the following questions.

- Will it be funny or serious? Educational, or just a bit of fun?
- How will you choose the people taking part? Will they know each other?
- What exactly will the contestants have to do? Give lots of examples.
- Where will the action take place? In a studio, or at different locations?
- Will it have the same people each time, or will they be different?
- Will there be a competition, with judges and voting, or some other way of finding a winner?
- Will there be prizes? What, and for whom?
- How long will each programme be?
- How will it be better than other similar programmes?

3 Explain your ideas

a Decide how you should present your ideas to the class. Do you need to show them an example of what will happen? How are you going to answer the questions above?

b Present your ideas to the class.

4 Choose and discuss

a In your group, discuss the good and bad points about the other groups' ideas, and choose your favourite.

b As a class, take turns to explain which programme your group thinks would be most successful, and why.

Speaking exercises: Student B

Unit 2, page 17, Exercise 8

Student B: Complete the questions with *say* or *tell*. Then ask your partner the questions.

1 Can you _____ your name backwards?
2 Have you ever _____ something out loud at the wrong time?
3 Can you _____ me a secret?
4 Do your parents always know when you're not _____ the truth?
5 When was the last time your parents _____ you off, and what was it for?

Unit 3, page 23, Exercise 6b

Are you a loyal friend?

Mostly a answers
You get on well with your friends, but when things get tough you disappear. Do you always let your friends down like this?

Mostly b answers
When it comes to loyalty, you stand by your friends in any situation. Are you sometimes a little too trusting?

Mostly c answers
You know how to balance loyalty with honesty – real friends want to know the truth, even when it hurts, don't they?

Unit 4, page 30, Exercise 8

Student B: Ask your partner for advice about these problems.

- You want to get a part-time job, but your parents don't want you to.
- You borrowed a friend's T-shirt, and now there's a big food stain on it.
- You got a message from someone who likes you, but you don't know who it is.
- Now think of your own problem.

Unit 8, page 59, Exercise 8

Student B: On a piece of paper, write something:

- you started to do but gave up.
- you remember doing when you were ten years old.
- you stopped doing when you became a teenager.
- you love doing.

Irregular verbs

Irregular verbs

Base form	Past simple	Past participle
be	was/were	been
beat	beat	beaten
become	became	become
begin	began	begun
blow	blew	blown
break	broke	broken
bring	brought	brought
build	built	built
buy	bought	bought
can	could	been able
catch	caught	caught
choose	chose	chosen
come	came	come
cost	cost	cost
cut	cut	cut
do	did	done
drink	drank	drunk
drive	drove	driven
eat	ate	eaten
fall	fell	fallen
feel	felt	felt
fight	fought	fought
find	found	found
fly	flew	flown
forget	forgot	forgotten
get	got	got
give	gave	given
go	went	gone
grow	grew	grown
have	had	had
hear	heard	heard
hit	hit	hit
hold	held	held
hurt	hurt	hurt
keep	kept	kept
know	knew	known
leave	left	left
let	let	let
lose	lost	lost
make	made	made
meet	met	met
pay	paid	paid
put	put	put
read	read	read
ride	rode	ridden
ring	rang	rung
run	ran	run
say	said	said
see	saw	seen
sell	sold	sold
send	sent	sent
shut	shut	shut
sing	sang	sung
sink	sank	sunk
sit	sat	sat

Base form	Past simple	Past participle
sleep	slept	slept
speak	spoke	spoken
spend	spent	spent
stand	stood	stood
steal	stole	stolen
swim	swam	swum
take	took	taken
teach	taught	taught
tell	told	told
think	thought	thought
understand	understood	understood
wake	woke	woken
wear	wore	worn
win	won	won
write	wrote	written

Phonetic symbols

Consonants		Vowels	
/p/	pen	/æ/	man
/b/	be	/ɑː/	father
/t/	two	/e/	ten
/d/	do	/ɜː/	thirteen
/k/	can	/ə/	mother
/g/	good	/ɪ/	sit
/f/	five	/iː/	see
/v/	very	/ʊ/	book
/m/	make	/uː/	food
/n/	nice	/ʌ/	up
/ŋ/	sing	/ɒ/	hot
/s/	see	/ɔː/	four
/z/	trousers		
/w/	we		
/l/	listen		
/r/	right		
/j/	you		
/h/	he		
/θ/	thing		
/ð/	this		
/ʃ/	she		
/tʃ/	cheese		
/ʒ/	usually		
/dʒ/	German		

Diphthongs	
/eɪ/	great
/aɪ/	fine
/ɔɪ/	boy
/ɪə/	hear
/eə/	chair
/aʊ/	town
/əʊ/	go
/ʊə/	pure

Thanks and acknowledgements

The authors would like to thank a number of people whose support has proved invaluable during the planning, writing and production process of the second edition of *English in Mind*:

The numerous teachers and students in many countries of the world who have used the first edition of *English in Mind*. Their enthusiasm for the course, and the detailed feedback and valuable suggestions we got from many of them, have been an important source of inspiration and guidance for us in the development and creation of the second edition. We would also like to thank those teachers who gave up their valuable time for interviews and focus groups.

Our editorial and production team for their cooperative spirit, their many excellent suggestions and their dedication, which have been characteristic of the entire editorial process: Stephanie Collins, Charlotte Aldis, Hannah Thacker, Flavia Lamborghini, Sophie Clarke, Michael Stubblefield, Angela Page, Laura Clyde, Helen Kenyon, Michelle Simpson and last but not least, James Dingle.

The team at Pentacor for giving the book its design; Anne Rosenfeld for the audio recordings; Caroline Jeffries and Sophie Finston at Lightning Pictures for the DVD; Hazel Meek, Eoin Higgins, Vanessa Manhire, for their excellent editorial support; and all the other people involved in this course.

The teams of educational consultants, representatives and managers working for Cambridge University Press in various countries around the world.

The leadership team at Cambridge University Press for the spirit of innovation that they have managed to instil in the Press, and for a constructive dialogue over the years: Ron Ragsdale, David Harrison, Hanri Pieterse and Stephen Bourne.

Last but not least, we would like to thank our partners, Mares and Adriana, for their support.

The authors and publishers acknowledge the following sources of copyright material and are grateful for the permissions granted. While every effort has been made, it has not always been possible to identify the sources of all the material used, or to trace all copyright holders. If any omissions are brought to our notice, we will be happy to include the appropriate acknowledgements on reprinting:

Cambridge University Press for the text on p.32 * 'The Book of Thoughts' from *The Fruitcake Special and Other Stories* by Frank Brennan. Copyright © 2000 Cambridge University Press, for the text on p.60 * 'Water of Wanting' from *Tasty Tales* by Frank Brennan;

Live Forever on p.38. Words and music by Noel Gallagher. Copyright © Copyright 1994 Creation Songs Limited/Oasis Music (GB). Sony/ATV Music Publishing (UK) Limited. All Rights Reserved. International Copyright Secured. Bell Voice Recordings for the sound a-like recording.

The publishers are grateful to the following for permission to reproduce copyright photographs and material:

Key: l = left, c = centre, r = right, t = top, b = bottom

Alamy pp6, 10, 11(l), 11(r), 15, 18, 22, 23(c), 23(t), 26(l), 26(r), 28(a), 28(b), 28(c), 28(cr), 28(f), 28(h), 28(tr), 30(cr), 30(r), 33, 40, 44(a), 44(b), 44(c), 44(d), 44(e), 44(f), 46(bl), 46(br), 46(tl), 46(tr), 48(b), 48(l), 48(r), 48(t), 56(a), 56(b), 56(c), 61, 69(l), 69(r); Corbis UK Ltd. pp28(e), 28(g), 30(l); Electronic Arts UK p58(cl); Getty Images pp39; iStockphoto pp23(b), 30(cl); Nintendo UK p58(t); Photolibrary Group pp56(d); Press Association Images pp12; Rex Features pp14, 28(b), 28(d), 42, 43, 70; Sony Computer Entertainment Europe pp58(bl),58(cr); Ubisoft Entertainment Ltd p58(br).

The publishers are grateful to the following illustrators:

Dan Chernett (Bright Agency), Rob Clarke (Three in a Box), Rosa Dodd (NB Illustration), Dylan Gibson, Ben Hasler (NB Illustration), David Haughey (Three in a Box), Tracey Knight (Lemonade Illustration), Anna Lazareva (Lemonade Illustration), Rob McClurkan, Tim Marrs (CIA), Pat Murray (Graham Cameron), Martin O'Neill (Debut Art), Mark Reihell (Lemonade Illustration), Ben Swift (NB Illustration), Jo Szachowska (Three in a Box), Russ Willms (Three in a Box),

The publishers are grateful to the following contributors:

Pentacor plc: text design, layouts and cover design

Zooid Pictures Ltd: photo research

Anne Rosenfeld and Dave Morritt: audio recordings

Julie Moore: Get it right! section

Commissioned photography (photo stories and cover): Alex Medeville

English in Mind

Second edition

Herbert Puchta & Jeff Stranks
with Richard Carter & Peter Lewis-Jones

Combo 3A
Workbook

CAMBRIDGE UNIVERSITY PRESS

1 Welcome

A

1 Present simple vs. present continuous

Complete the sentences. Use the present simple or present continuous form of the verbs.

I'm Christy Bell, and I'm in Year 11 at a school in Manchester. This is my big GCSE exam year, so I ¹ *don't have* (not have) as much free time as I did before. When I ² _____ (not do) my homework or studying for tests, I try to see my friends. Saturday night is really the only time when everyone's free, because most of my friends ³ _____ (work) on Saturdays. I have a job in a home and garden centre, but now it ⁴ _____ (get) harder to find enough time to do that and all of my school work too. I ⁵ _____ (need) the money, though, because I don't get any pocket money from my mum. I ⁶ _____ (do) some babysitting, which is good because I usually ⁷ _____ (get) my school work done at the same time, and I get paid for it!

Most of the boys in my class seem to spend a lot of their free time on computers. More and more of them ⁸ _____ (get) computer games, or doing online gaming, but I don't like them much. And these days people ⁹ _____ (use) instant messaging to talk to friends, but I ¹⁰ _____ (prefer) texting my friends on my mobile – I hate sitting in front of a computer for hours. I do enough of that with my homework!!

2 Question tags

Complete each question tag. Write one word in each space.

1 He's just a child, *isn't* he?
2 It isn't easy being a teenager, _____ it?
3 They're only 3 and 4 years old – they're just toddlers, _____ they?
4 Leaving a tap on wastes water, _____ it?
5 You recycled that paper, _____ you?
6 We can't go on destroying the rainforests, _____ we?
7 Your sister's just had a baby, _____ she?
8 We shouldn't drop litter on the streets, _____ we?
9 The atmosphere's become very polluted, _____ it?
10 One day you'll be a pensioner, _____ you?

3 Describing someone's age and the environment

Find twelve words in the wordsnake. Write them in the correct columns.

wastechildtoddlerforestfumesbabylitteratmosphereteenagerpensionerrecycleyoungadultrubbish

Ages	Environment
	waste

UNIT 1

B

1 Ways of talking about the future

a Read the sentences. Mark them *A* if it is an arrangement, *P* if it is a prediction or *I* if it is an intention.

1 'I've decided on a subject to study at university – Biology.' *I*
2 'We've arranged to visit my grandparents on Saturday.'
3 'My dad? Give me money to buy a new computer? Definitely not!'
4 'I phoned the doctor and made an appointment to see her tomorrow morning.'
5 'Planes fly from London to Australia in ten hours in the future? Yes, definitely.'
6 'My friend Mike has decided to leave school next year.'

b Use the underlined words in Exercise 1b to make sentences: for arrangement use present continuous; for prediction use *will/won't*; for intention use *going to*.

1 *I'm going to study Biology at university.*
2 ....
3 ....
4 ....
5 ....
6 ....

2 Musical instruments

Match the words with the pictures. Write a–f in the boxes.

1 keyboards *e*
2 trumpet
3 drums
4 piano
5 flute
6 guitar

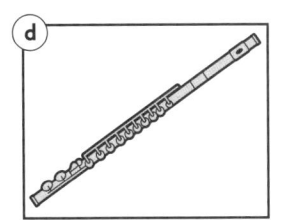

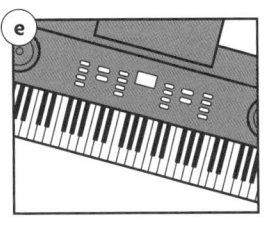

3 Medicine and health

Circle the correct words.

1 He fell over in town and broke his leg. An *(ambulance) / injection* took him to hospital.
2 I went to the doctor and she gave me *a surgeon / an injection*.
3 If you carry that heavy bag, you might *hurt / pain* yourself.
4 I hit my leg this morning, and now it's really *hurt / sore*.
5 Thousands of people are ill – it's a big *epidemic / cold*.
6 She's got a headache and a very high *temperature / pain*.
7 My uncle had to see the doctor because of the *sore / pain* in his back.
8 Some doctors in Britain complain that they've got too many *injections / patients*.

C

1 Present perfect simple with *for* or *since*

a Complete the sentences with *for* or *since*.

1. Pietro has been in England ___since___ the start of the summer.
2. He has studied English _____ he was seven years old.
3. His mother has been with him in England _____ two weeks.
4. He hasn't eaten any fish and chips _____ he arrived.
5. He hasn't had a good cup of coffee _____ he left Italy.
6. He hasn't seen his friends _____ a long time.

b Make sentences with the present perfect of the underlined verb and *for* or *since*.

1. I <u>have</u> a bicycle. My parents gave it to me last year.   *I've had my bicycle for a year / since last year.*
2. I'<u>m</u> in this class. I joined the class six months ago.   _____
3. Joanna and I <u>are</u> friends. We became friends in 2009.   _____
4. I <u>know</u> Paul Carpenter. I first met him a year ago.   _____

2 British vs. American English

Sally is a British teenager. She's writing to her new American friend, Mina. Find eight words (one on each line) that Mina might not understand. Change them into American English.

Hi Mina

My name's Sally and I'm going to tell you about myself. I live in London. Our ~~flat~~   _apartment_
is on the tenth floor so we have to go up in a lift to get to it! The place where we live is OK   _____
but unfortunately a lot of people around here throw rubbish on the street instead of putting   _____
it in the bin, so the pavements get dirty and that's not really very nice, is it? Anyway, what   _____
else can I tell you? Well, I like sport a lot, especially football, but I don't play it, I just watch   _____
it on TV. I think perhaps I should do some sport because I eat a lot! I just love biscuits and   _____
most days I eat a lot of sweets too, so I'm not the healthiest person in the world! Starting   _____
next week, though, I'm going to start cycling to school (now I use the underground), so that   _____
will help me to get fit, I hope!
Write soon and tell me about yourself, OK?! Bye!

3 Homes

Match the words and their definitions. Write a–f in the boxes.

1. detached — c
2. garage
3. garden
4. flat
5. lift
6. caravan

a. a machine that takes you from one floor to another
b. a 'house' on wheels
c. not connected to other houses
d. a place to keep cars
e. an area near a house with grass and flowers
f. a home on one floor of a large building

D

1 used to

Look at the information about people who have changed things in their lives. Write sentences.

name	in the past	now
Paul	meat	fish
Sandra	tea	coffee
Amanda	dog	cat
June	magazines	newspapers
Gregory	car	bicycle
Daniel	TV	sport

1 (eat) *Paul used to eat meat, but now he eats fish.*
2 (drink) ....
3 (have) ....
4 (read) ....
5 (drive/ride) ....
6 (watch/play) ....

2 mustn't vs. don't have to

Circle the correct words.

1 You *don't have to* / mustn't drive fast – we've got lots of time.
2 You *don't have to* / *mustn't* drive fast – this road is full of holes and very dangerous.
3 You *don't have to* / *mustn't* buy a new laptop – they're much too expensive.
4 You *don't have to* / *mustn't* buy a new laptop – I can fix your old one easily.
5 You *don't have to* / *mustn't* tell Sarah about the party – I invited her last night.
6 You *don't have to* / *mustn't* tell James about the party – I really don't want him to know about it!
7 You *don't have to* / *mustn't* get up today – it's a holiday!
8 You *don't have to* / *mustn't* get up today – the doctor told me to stay in bed.
9 You *don't have to* / *mustn't* wash my new shirt – it can only be dry-cleaned.
10 You *don't have to* / *mustn't* wash my new shirt – it isn't dirty.

3 Information technology

Complete the crossword puzzle.

1 With a laptop, you can use a mouse or a touch ___pad___ .
2 Find the programme on the internet and then ___ it – it's free!
3 I couldn't type anything – the ___ was broken!
4 To access this site, you need to log ___ first.
5 I had to buy a new power ___ for my laptop.
6 Put the CD into the ___ and it will run automatically.
7 My dad just installed a new wi-fi ___ at home.
8 How many USB ___ has this computer got?
9 I remember my username – but I can't remember the ___ !

UNIT 1

2 Communication

1 Grammar
★ Past simple vs. present perfect simple

a Complete the dialogues. Use the past simple or the present perfect simple form of the verbs.

1 **Anton:** _Have_ you two _met_ (meet) before?
   Lauren: Yes. We both _went_ (go) to that party last week.

2 **Setsuko:** How long .... you .... (know) Marek?
   Andrej: We .... (meet) on the first day of this course.

3 **Callum:** .... you .... (see) any films last weekend?
   Shayla: No. I .... (not go) to the cinema for ages.

4 **Ramon:** .... you .... (finish) that Harry Potter book yet?
   Tessa: Oh, yes, I .... (take) it back to the library yesterday.

5 **Jay:** .... you .... (speak) to Will yesterday?
   Soraya: No, I .... (not see) him for a couple of days.

6 **Carrie:** .... you .... (buy) Lee's birthday present yet?
   Jen: Yes, I .... (get) her something in town last night.

7 **Shandra:** When .... you .... (learn) to drive?
   Jack: Me? I .... (never drive) a car in my life.

b Complete the questions. Use the past simple or present perfect simple.

1 **A:** I've got really bad toothache.
   B: Oh, I'm sorry. How long _have you had it_?

2 **A:** We don't live in Hutton Avenue any more.
   B: Oh, I didn't know that. When ....?

3 **A:** We had a great time at the cinema last night.
   B: Oh, really? What film ....?

4 **A:** I lived in Japan when I was younger.
   B: That's interesting. How long .... there?

5 **A:** I'm working part-time in a restaurant.
   B: Oh, yeah? When ....?

6 **A:** So you've finally arrived!
   B: Sorry I'm late! How long .... here?

c Complete the sentences with the present simple, past simple and present perfect simple forms of the verbs.

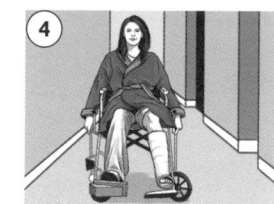

1 I _know_ Pete. I .... him for years. In fact, our grandfathers .... each other when they were alive. (know)

2 He .... at this restaurant since last summer. He .... in the kitchen. Before that, he .... in a shop. (work)

3 When she was younger, she .... in Russia. Now she .... in Japan. She .... there for five years. (live)

4 I .... my leg. I .... it on a skiing trip last month. I .... something every time I ski. (break)

80 UNIT 2

d Read the diary of a woman who went to a seminar to learn how to talk to animals. Some of the lines have a word that should not be there. Write the word at the end of the line, or tick (✔) if the line is correct.

I arrived here last night. Today we all paid our fee, $160 for an eight-hour	1 ✔
workshop. Then we got to know our trainer, a woman ~~is~~ called Claire.	2 *is*
'I've had have horses since my childhood,' she said. 'But it took me a	3
long while to find out that I can understand them! You can to learn this too.	4
Animals talk all the time. You just need to learn to listen to them.' After	5
breakfast we have worked in pairs. 'Close your eyes, think of a message	6
and communicate it through your thoughts,' said Claire. I decided	7
to 'tell' to my partner that 'The mountain is purple.' After two minutes of	8
concentration (I got a headache) she told for me what she understood: 'It's	9
too hot in here!' Well, never mind, we're here to read the thoughts of	10
animals, not humans! After lunch, we did sat on the grass near Claire's	11
horses and closed our eyes. Half an hour since later we went back to the	12
house. So what messages did we have read? 'It's hot.' 'We like the grass.'	13
Do I really need an animal communicator to learn that a horses like grass?	14

✱ Time expressions

e Two time expressions are correct, and one is incorrect. ~~Cross out~~ the incorrect answer.
1 Have you called your mother *already / yet / ~~yesterday~~*?
2 Philip has *already / just* left school *in 2004*.
3 We didn't have time to clean up *last night / already / before* we left.
4 Actually, I saw that film *two days ago / just / on Sunday*.
5 They've *never* seen snow *last winter / already*.
6 I haven't heard from Mike *since the party / for a few days / about a week ago*.
7 We had an old black Beetle *when I was little / since the 80s / for about ten years*.

f Rewrite the sentences using the words in brackets.
1 I've known Mrs Craig for four years. (met)
   I met Mrs Craig four years ago.
2 Jessica bought her mobile phone last week. (for)
3 William called a minute ago. (just)
4 How long have you had that bag? (buy)
5 Your friends have been here for an hour. (ago)
6 Your birthday cards got here yesterday. (since)
7 The last time I saw you was at your party. (haven't)

2 Pronunciation
✱ Sentence stress

a Read the sentences. Underline the words that are stressed. Sometimes there is more than one possibility.
1 How long have you had it?
2 When did you move?
3 What film did you see?
4 How long did you live there?
5 When did you start working there?
6 How long have you been here?

b ▶ CD2 T7 Listen, check and repeat.

3 Vocabulary

★ Body language

a Match the two parts of the sentences. Write a–j in the boxes.

1. That guy's leaning — *i*
2. Could you try to make
3. Just sit
4. If you agree, nod
5. Just try to avoid
6. She's fantastic – she always gives
7. Try not to look
8. Did you just raise
9. I see you've just folded
10. What do you think she's gesturing

a. back in your chair and enjoy this film.
b. you that warm smile when you walk in the room.
c. your eyebrows at me? Is there a problem?
d. nervous, even if you feel it!
e. eye contact with the waiter? I need some water.
f. eye contact if you don't want to talk to him.
g. about? Do you think she's in trouble?
h. your arms. I hope you're not getting impatient with me.
i. forward a lot – do you think he's trying to listen to us?
j. your head three times.

★ *say* and *tell*

b Complete the sentences with the correct form of *say* or *tell*.

1. I can't ___tell___ the difference between the new version and the old one.
2. If something is bothering you, please _____ it out loud – don't whisper to your friends.
3. He's only two years old, but he can already _____ the time.
4. Can I _____ you a secret if you promise to keep it to yourself?
5. I hope you're not _____ me a lie. You'll be in trouble if you are.
6. I'm sure you've _____ me that joke before. Don't you know any others?

c Complete the sentences with the correct form of *say* or *tell* and one of the expressions in the box.

> thank you   sorry   goodbye   ~~a prayer~~   you off   him a story   the truth   that again

1. I've got a job interview this afternoon, so I need some luck. Will you ___say a prayer___?
2. Ouch! That really hurt! Aren't you going to _____?
3. Sorry, I didn't hear you. Could you _____?
4. I don't believe you! Are you sure you're _____?
5. That's a really nice present your grandma sent you. You need to write and _____.
6. He won't go to sleep until you _____.
7. Well, that's the end of the class. It's time to _____.
8. Look what you've done! Wait until your dad sees this – he's really going to _____.

d **Vocabulary bank** Replace the underlined words with a phrase from the box. Write a–j in the boxes.

> a talks nonsense b talk back c speak a word of d on speaking terms e talk sport
> f Talk about g ~~spoke too soon~~ h Speak up i speak your mind j talking shop

1 Mum said it wasn't going to rain, but she said that without thinking. The sky's full of dark clouds. [g]

2 I can't hear a word you're saying. Talk more loudly, please. ☐

3 Alex, don't reply rudely to the teacher like that! ☐

4 I only spoke English when I was on holiday in Spain, because I can't say anything at all in Spanish. ☐

5 I'd like you to tell me exactly what you think. ☐

6 I don't want to go out with Tom and his friends – they just discuss things like football all the time. ☐

7 You can't believe a word that Jason says. He says stupid things all the time! ☐

8 I've just read this book. It's absolutely fantastic! You really must read it. ☐

9 Dad loves discussing work with his colleagues. ☐

10 Francesca and Ally have argued again. They aren't communicating with each other at all at the moment. ☐

4 Culture in mind

Read the text. Then mark the statements *T* (true), *F* (false) or *N* (not enough information).

1 Africans used drumming before Europeans discovered the continent. ☐

2 Slaves used drumming to send messages about their slave masters. ☐

3 Slave masters encouraged the use of drumming. ☐

4 Some drumming sounds a bit like speech. ☐

5 Drumming communication differs from one country to another. ☐

6 People add new words and phrases to the drumming 'language' all the time. ☐

7 About half of all drum messages are misunderstood. ☐

Talking Drums

In some parts of Africa, drums have been used for communication for hundreds of years. That was how, for example, tribes knew that European explorers were on their way – they heard the drum messages from miles away, long before the explorers actually appeared. At one time, drums were banned, because slaves were using them to send messages to each other. The slave masters couldn't understand the messages and were worried about what the slaves were 'saying', so they banned the use of the drums.

There are three types of drumming. One type uses rhythms to send a particular signal. A second type of drumming repeats the patterns of speech (i.e. it matches the rhythm of specific words or sentences). And the third type is more musical. None of the forms of drumming are proper languages. Indeed, there is no international drumming language at all. Drum communication is localised and quite limited. People can't suddenly add new expressions to the drumming, so it can't be used to say anything you want. And there is always a danger that messages will be misunderstood. Nevertheless, drumming is still a valuable way of sending limited information, where the people who hear it understand the message.

UNIT 2 83

Skills in mind

5 Write

a Read this email to Laura from her friend Nadia.

To: lauranichols@easymail.com
From: n.stephens@dphigh.edu

Hey girl! Just a quick email to tell you I'm still alive! Mum said I can't use my phone this month, 'cos I spent too much last month.

Oh, well. Listen – email me back.
– How's your week been?
– Any luck with finding a job?
– Things OK with Tom?
– Ian Finch's party!! It's tomorrow night. Are we meeting there?
– Any other news I should know about?

Write back soon!

Love, Nadia

---

b Read Laura's reply. Does she answer all of Nadia's questions? What is wrong with the underlined phrases?

c Replace the underlined phrases above with phrases a–f below. Write 1–6 in the boxes.

a Things are going well with Tom   3
b So, about
c Hi Nadia,
d He's still not sure about
e Take care
f I don't really want to do that

WRITING TIP

Using appropriate language

When you write a letter or an email, it is very important to choose language that is appropriate for the reader.

- Think about who the letter is for. If it is someone you already know (a friend or a pen-friend, for example), then your language can be more simple and informal.

- Make sure you include all the information you are asked to include, in a natural way.

- When you learn new words and expressions, ask your teacher if they are formal or informal. If you learn the way to start a formal letter, also find out how to start a letter to a pen-friend, for example.

To: n.stephens@dphigh.edu
From: lauranichols@easymail.com

¹Dear Ms Stephens,

How's things? Sorry to hear about your 'phone problem'! How are you going to survive without your mobile? Anyway, my week's been OK – the usual stuff at college. I think I'll stay, though. I can't find any music jobs except working in the megastore at the shopping centre, and ²that is not a suitable option for the rest of my life.

³My relationship with Tom is proceeding well – he's been really sweet recently. ⁴He has not made a decision so far regarding going to university next year. I think he should go, even if it means we'll be apart. Decisions, decisions!

⁵With reference to Ian's party – we could meet up before, if you want. How about Starblast Coffee at 7.30?

Guess who we bumped into today? Ben Davis – he's back from Hong Kong. He seems a bit unhappy – his parents have broken up and he's not sure what he wants to do. He's coming to the party. You used to like Ben, didn't you?

⁶Yours faithfully,

Love Laura

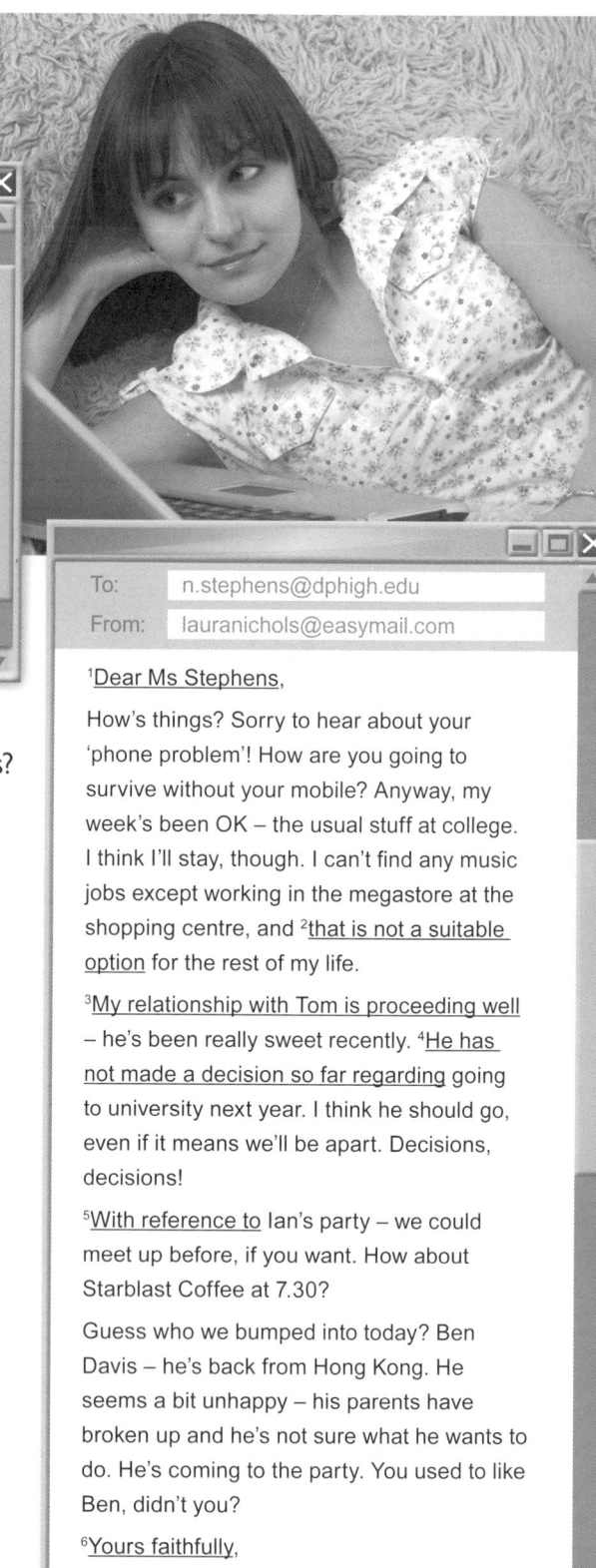

d Write a similar 120-word email from Rebecca to Kylie in which she passes on her latest news. Use the information from Exercise 12 on page 19 of the Student's Book.

Unit check

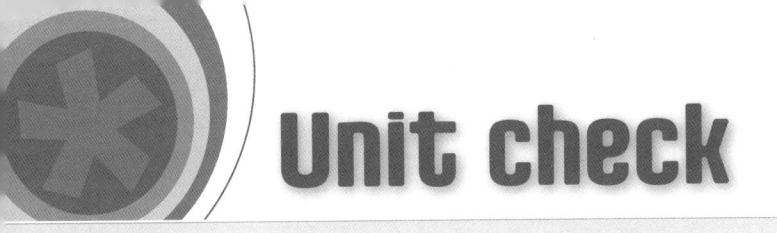

1 Fill in the spaces

Complete the text with the words in the box.

back   nod   make   ~~gesturing~~   telling   eye   forward   warm   look   arms

It's funny how different people communicate in groups. Some people are always _gesturing_ with their hands, and others just stand with their [1]_____ folded. Some talk non-stop, and others just sit [2]_____ and [3]_____ their heads occasionally. I have a problem with people who don't [4]_____ eye contact. When someone doesn't look at you, it looks like they're [5]_____ lies, especially when they [6]_____ nervous too. It's funny — you can give someone a [7]_____ smile, but they still avoid [8]_____ contact. It makes me want to lean [9]_____ and say, 'Hey, it's me, I'm talking to you!'

☐ 9

2 Choose the correct answers

Circle the correct answer: a, b or c.

1. I've _____ made a terrible mistake.
   a yet   b ever   c (just)
2. She _____ seen her boyfriend all week.
   a never   b didn't   c hasn't
3. I _____ run to college in the mornings — it's only two kilometres.
   a haven't   b usually   c didn't
4. Wait! I haven't had breakfast _____ .
   a still   b ago   c yet
5. How long _____ you wait for me last night?
   a did   b have   c do
6. I can't believe your mum didn't _____ off for taking the car without asking.
   a say you   b tell   c tell you
7. My birthday was three days _____ .
   a ago   b just   c last
8. My brother and sister _____ bought me a present for my birthday.
   a didn't yet   b has never   c still haven't
9. You haven't _____ sorry for shouting at me.
   a say   b saying   c said

☐ 8

3 Vocabulary

Choose the correct word.

Our parents have always encouraged us to speak our [1]_____ . But that doesn't mean they want us to talk [2]_____ . They [3]_____ right away if we ever do that, and they tell us [4]_____ for doing it. They don't like it if we talk [5]_____ to them, either. Mum tried to give my brother a [6]_____ about that the other day but he [7]_____ off into his room, so he got away that time! Mum says good manners are important. We have to say 'please' and 'thank you', and we have to say it out [8]_____ so everyone hears us.

1. a words   b minds   c memories   d voices
2. a nonsense   b lies   c truth   d silly
3. a believe   b reply   c tell   d notice
4. a in   b out   c off   d up
5. a from   b to   c at   d back
6. a sign   b warning   c telling   d saying
7. a charged   b ranged   c signed   d hid
8. a noisy   b wide   c loud   d big

☐ 8

How did you do?

Total: ☐ 25

| ☺ Very good 20 – 25 | ☹ OK 14 – 19 | ☹ Review Unit 2 again 0 – 13 |

3 A true friend

1 Grammar

★ Past simple vs. past continuous review

a Complete the sentences with the past simple or past continuous form of the verbs.

1 While I *was looking* (look) for my tennis balls, I *found* (find) an old sandwich under my bed.
2 When my parents _____ (come) back, we _____ (have) a party.
3 When I _____ (open) the door, they _____ (dance) in the dark.
4 I _____ (find) this girl's phone number while I _____ (clean) your room.
5 While we _____ (wait), we _____ (start) to write the invitations.
6 I _____ (teach) a gym class when I _____ (hear) about the plane crash.
7 Someone _____ (call) you on your mobile while you _____ (take) the dog for a walk.

b Complete the sentences with the past simple or past continuous form of the verbs.

Godzilla the cat had a special relationship with her owner, David Hart. David often *went* (go) away for work. While he ¹_____ (travel), his mother ²_____ (come) over to his house to look after the cat. One day while the telephone ³_____ (ring), his mother ⁴_____ (notice) Godzilla get up off the sofa and sit down next to the phone. She ⁵_____ (pick) up the phone. It was David. The next time the phone ⁶_____ (ring), Godzilla ⁷_____ (do) the same thing. It was David again. But the next time, Godzilla ⁸_____ (not move). His mother ⁹_____ (answer) the phone – it wasn't David. She started to notice that every time David ¹⁰_____ (phone), Godzilla ¹¹_____ (go) to sit next to the phone. When it wasn't David, Godzilla ¹²_____ (stay) where she was.

★ Time conjunctions: as / then / as soon as

c Connect the sentences with the words in brackets. Sometimes you need to change the order of the sentences.

1 His parents came to stay at his house. David went away to work. (when)
  When David went away to work, his parents came to stay at his house.
2 The phone started ringing. Godzilla ran and sat next to the phone. (as soon as)
  _____
3 The hall light came on. She was parking her car. (as)
  _____
4 The dog started barking. I got to the gate. (as soon as)
  _____
5 Sometimes an animal starts behaving strangely. Something happens to its owner. (then)
  _____
6 Many animals are waiting at the door. Their owners are still travelling home. (as)
  _____

2 Pronunciation

★ Linking sounds

a Look at the way these words from Exercise 1b are linked:

her‿owner   David‿often
went‿away   look‿after

b ▶ CD2 T8 Mark similar links in the text, then listen and check.

3 Grammar

★ Past simple vs. past perfect simple

a Match the sentence halves. Write a–d in the boxes.

1 A man was arrested for a bank robbery after police called him on his mobile phone. The man ...
2 A man was arrested in hospital for trying to steal money from a house safe after police found his glove at the house. The safe ...
3 A man who had climbed Mount Everest six times died as a result of a fall at home. He ...
4 An unemployed man who tried to print his own money was caught as soon as he tried to spend it. He ...

a had used black ink on the notes instead of green, because he was colour-blind.
b had left a business card at the bank with his phone number on it.
c had fallen on his hand and cut off one of his fingers. The man ran away, leaving his glove behind. When the man went to hospital with a missing finger, the police were able to match the finger to the hand.
d had climbed a ladder to change a light bulb in the kitchen when he fell and cracked his head on the sink.

b Complete the sentences. Use the past perfect and the past simple or past continuous form of the verbs.

1 As soon as he ___closed___ (close) the door, he _____ (realise) that he _____ (leave) his key inside.
2 I _____ (have) the feeling that I _____ (meet) her somewhere before.
3 I _____ (not know) what I _____ (say) to her, but she _____ (cry).
4 They _____ (get) to the cinema ten minutes after the film _____ (start).
5 My mobile _____ (not work) because I _____ (forget) to charge it.
6 I _____ (see) you sitting and smiling half an hour before the end of the exam. _____ you already _____ (finish)?

c Read the text about the American TV show *Friends*. Some of the lines have a word that should not be there. The extra words are connected to tenses. Write the incorrect extra word at the end of the line, or tick (✔) if the line is correct.

Friends is still ~~being~~ one of the most popular TV shows in the world,   1 ___being___
even after they stopped making it in 2004. The show had had three   2 ___✔___
previous names before it had became simply *Friends*: *Friends Like Us*,   3 _____
Across The Hall and *Six Of One*, but in the end one word was been   4 _____
enough. Apart from the six main characters, the only other person to   5 _____
appear in all ten years that they have made the show was Gunther, the   6 _____
coffee shop server. He was having the only person in the cast that knew   7 _____
how to operate a cappuccino machine.
Why was the show so popular? It was being usually well written and   8 _____
funny, of course, but what has kept fans watching for more than a decade   9 _____
is possibly the fact that the group of six always did stayed friends, no   10 _____
matter what were problems the characters had on screen, or the actors   11 _____
had in real life.

4 Vocabulary

★ Friends and enemies

a Replace the underlined words with a phrase from the box. Write a–f in the boxes.

> a let me down   b fallen out   c ~~tell on me~~   d stand by you   e get on well with
> f sticking up for me

1 Please don't <u>tell anyone that I did it</u>! I'll be your friend forever! — c
2 Your most loyal friends are the ones who <u>stay loyal to you</u> in the bad times.
3 Thanks for <u>supporting me</u> in there. I thought nobody was going to agree with me.
4 You really <u>have a good relationship with</u> your stepbrothers and stepsisters, don't you?
5 It looks like Darren and Varsha have <u>stopped being friends</u>. They don't talk to each other any more.
6 You said you would go with me! Please don't <u>disappoint me</u> – I don't want to go alone.

b Look at the pictures. Choose a phrase from the box in Exercise 4a to complete sentences 1–5 below. There is one phrase you won't need.

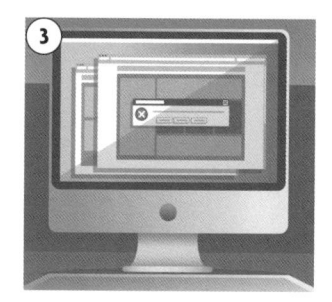

c **Vocabulary bank** Complete the sentences with the words in the box.

> allies   acquaintance   ~~old~~   hit it off
> mate   make   friends   are for   close

1 I've known Arthur for a very long time – we're ___old___ friends.
2 The two countries were _____ during the war.
3 He's very shy – it isn't easy for him to _____ friends with people.
4 We met, he liked me and I liked him – we _____ immediately!
5 They know all of each other's secrets and so on – they're really _____ friends.
6 This is Alex – he's a _____ of mine from our school days.
7 She isn't a friend really, just a business _____ of my mother's.
8 You don't have to thank me – that's what _____ , after all.

1 Oh, no! What have I done? Look, don't __c__ and I'll give you some of my sweets.
2 It's amazing that they _____ each other.
3 Come on, come on! Please don't _____ now!
4 Phew! Thanks for _____ .
5 Oh, no! It looks like they've _____ with each other. Be careful what you say.

UNIT 3

5 Everyday English

a Complete the expressions with the words in the box.

then   could   ~~especially~~   sooner   news   matter

1 A: Do you like Chinese food?
   B: Not _especially_.

2 A: Dan hasn't invited you to his party.
   B: Well, I won't invite him to mine, _____.

3 A: Do you mind if I copy your homework?
   B: As a _____ of fact I do. Do it yourself.

4 A: Are you going to Diana's party?
   B: Party? That's _____ to me. I didn't know she was having one.

5 A: Mum, I'm sorry. I ate the last piece of cake.
   B: How _____ you? I was saving that for your dad.

6 A: When do you want our homework in, Sir?
   B: The _____ the better, but no later than Thursday.

b Complete the dialogue with the expressions from Exercise 5a.

Steve: Hey Brian, do you like MGMT?
Brian: ¹ _Not especially_, why?
Steve: They're playing at the Academy in May.
Brian: Really? ² _____. Are you going?
Steve: Absolutely. I bought my tickets yesterday.
Brian: Tickets?
Steve: Yes, one's for Jen. I've invited her along.
Brian: What! ³ _____? You know I like her.
Steve: So why don't you come along, ⁴ _____?
Brian: ⁵ _____ I think I will. When should I get my ticket?
Steve: ⁶ _____. They're selling really quickly.
Brian: OK, I'm going to buy mine now! See you.

6 Study help

* Using appropriate language

- When you learn new words and phrases, it is important to know if the language is formal or informal. For example, it is not appropriate to end a letter requesting information about a course with 'Take care'. At the same time, you can sound too formal if you write 'Yours faithfully' in an email to someone you met on a school exchange programme.

- Phrasal verbs are usually, but not always, more informal ways of saying something. It is fine to say to a friend 'Let's meet up sometime', but in a formal situation it would be better to say 'I would like to arrange an appointment for ...'.

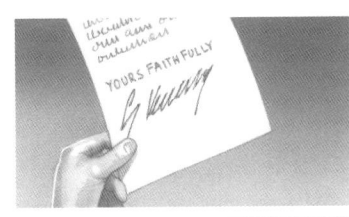

Skills in mind

7 Listen

a ▶ CD2 T9 Read statements A–C below. Then listen and read what the person says about pets and their owners. Decide which statement you think is the speaker's opinion.

A Pet owners have a special understanding with their animals.

B Only dogs have a telepathic relationship with their owners, not other pets.

C The 'special relationship' between a pet and its owner does not really exist.

> 'A lot of people seem to think that pets, especially dogs, are somehow telepathic. They think that they have a special understanding with their animal, so that for example, their pet knows when they are coming home, or knows when something is wrong. I think that's ridiculous, though. These things are just coincidence, or it's just that the owner is trying to 'wish' that their pet is special.'

Check your answer at the bottom of the page.

LISTENING TIP

Matching speakers with opinions

- In this kind of question, you will usually hear a number of different people talking about a similar subject.
- It is important to read the statements carefully first, to be clear about the differences between each one.
- The speakers may use different words from the ones in the statements, but the meaning will be the same.
- Try to think of other ways to express the ideas in the statements, to imagine what the speaker might say. For example, when the statement is 'It's not necessary', the speaker might say 'You don't have to' or 'You don't need to'.
- The speaker may seem to be agreeing with the statement because they use the same words, but actually go on to disagree with the statement and therefore think the opposite. For example, the speaker might say, '*Some people* think you have to see your best friend every day, *but I don't* think that's necessary.'
- Remember you are being asked for *the speaker's* opinion, not yours!

b ▶ CD2 T10 Listen to five people talking about best friends, and match each speaker with one of the options A–F. Use each letter only once. There is one extra letter you won't need.

Speaker 1 ☐   A It's not necessary to see your best friend every day.
Speaker 2 ☐   B You don't always like people the first time you meet them.
Speaker 3 ☐   C Some people don't have any friends.
Speaker 4 ☐   D It's not important to have a 'best' friend.
Speaker 5 ☐   E It's not so hard to make 'new best friends'.
                  F It's normal to fight with your best friend sometimes.

Answer: Statement C ('The speaker says 'A lot of people seem to think ...', but this probably does not include the speaker. The speaker also says 'especially dogs', which does not mean only dogs. The third and fourth sentences give the speaker's opinion: 'I think ...'.)

Unit check

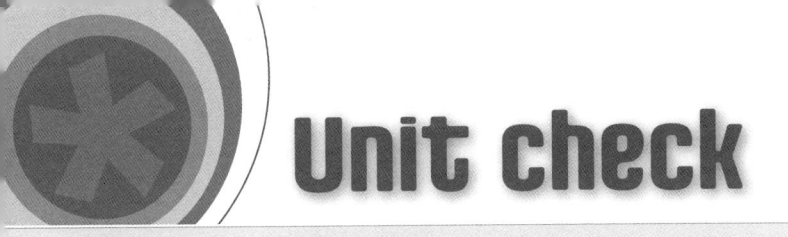

1 Fill in the spaces

Complete the text with the words in the box.

> loyalty ~~friendships~~ up out stood get letting had while friends

One of the great __friendships__ in literature is the one between the hobbits Frodo Baggins and Samwise Gamgee in *The Lord of the Rings*. Sam, who [1]_____ been Frodo's servant at their home in the Shire, accompanied Frodo and his company on a journey to destroy the ring and save the world. [2]_____ they were making their journey, Sam [3]_____ by his master through all kinds of danger, never [4]_____ him down. The story shows us that, even for people who [5]_____ on very well, there are times when our [6]_____ is tested and we can fall [7]_____ with each other. However, true [8]_____ always stick [9]_____ for each other in the end.

[9]

2 Choose the correct answers

Circle the correct answer: a, b or c.

1 You're not going to tell _____ her, are you?
   a well   b down   c (on)

2 Her old car never _____ her down.
   a makes   b does   c lets

3 _____ soon as we left, the snow started.
   a While   b As   c Then

4 I _____ already bought my tickets for the show before we got to the theatre.
   a have   b was   c had

5 Dogs are very _____ to their owners.
   a loyal   b friend   c stick

6 While she was having a shower, somebody _____ her towel.
   a stole   b had stolen   c was stealing

7 _____ my brother was born, we moved to a bigger house.
   a While   b When   c Then

8 My best friend and I fall _____ about twice a week, but we're soon friends again.
   a up   b out   c in

9 I _____ want to watch the film because I had seen it three times before.
   a hadn't   b didn't   c wasn't

[8]

3 Vocabulary

Circle the correct words.

1 A good friend will always stand *on* / *(by)* you, no matter what.

2 I think it's great the way you stick *up* / *out* for your friend.

3 He's not really a friend but more of a/an *acquaintance* / *mate* – someone I knew at school.

4 I get *on* / *up* really well with all my teachers. I really like them.

5 Ali and I *hit* / *fell* it off as soon as we met. We've been friends ever since.

6 She's a really *close* / *open* friend. I tell her everything.

7 You don't need to thank me. That's *why* / *what* friends are for.

8 She feels you really *let* / *threw* her down. That's why's she's upset with you.

9 If you hit me again I'm going to tell *on* / *out* you to the teacher.

[8]

How did you do?

Total: [25]

| 😊 Very good 20 – 25 | 😐 OK 14 – 19 | ☹ Review Unit 3 again 0 – 13 |

UNIT 3

4 A working life

1 Grammar
★ Present perfect simple vs. continuous review

a Circle the correct words.

1 Your brother has (written) / been writing three job applications this morning.
2 I've been doing / done an IT course at the weekends. I've got one more week to go.
3 I don't leave school for another year, but I've already started / been starting to look for a job.
4 Have you seen / been seeing the new James Bond film?
5 My dad has always had / been having a thick beard.
6 What do you mean, you haven't had time to make dinner! What have you done / been doing all evening?
7 It's snowed / been snowing all night. Do you think it'll stop by tomorrow morning?

b Complete the sentences with the words in the box.

| gone | been going | called | been calling |
| taken | been taking | painted | been painting |

1 Her French is getting much better. She's _been going_ to classes twice a week.
2 I've _____ three of the walls and both doors – just one more wall to go.
3 You've just _____ me! Did you forget to tell me something?
4 He's _____ out, I'm afraid. If you want to wait, he'll be back in an hour.
5 I've _____ photos for the last two hours. The camera doesn't have any memory left now.
6 Have you _____ in here? It certainly smells like it.
7 Alisha's _____ you all day. Where have you been?
8 Who has _____ the last piece of cake? I wanted it!

c Match the dialogues and pictures, then complete. Use the present perfect simple or continuous.

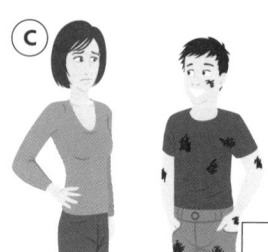

1 A: Where's your sister?
   B: She __'s gone__ out with her friend. (go)
2 A: You look terrible! What's wrong?
   B: Oh, I _____ (not sleep) well recently. Too much homework, I think!
3 A: Do you want another slice of this pizza? It's excellent.
   B: No, thanks. I _____ enough. (eat)
4 A: I'm so sorry I'm late! How long _____ you _____? (wait)
   B: Too long! I'm soaking wet.
5 A: What _____ you _____? (do)
   B: Helping Dad change a tyre on the car.
6 A: _____ you _____ (finish) the washing-up in there?
   B: No, not yet. _____ you _____ (see) how many dirty dishes there are?

92 UNIT 4

d Complete the questions. Use the present perfect simple or continuous form of the verbs in the box.

| do | have | go | download | save | know |

1. So is that your new boyfriend? How long _have you been going_ out with him?
2. Nice phone, Jake. How long _____ it?
3. I didn't know you could water ski! How long _____ that?
4. I hear you want to buy a new sound system. How long _____ for it?
5. You didn't tell me you'd passed all of your exams! How long _____ ?
6. That film file is huge! How long _____ it?

e Continue the biography of singer/songwriter Craig David using the information below. Use past simple and present perfect simple or continuous where appropriate.

- born in Southampton, England (1981)
- started singing and DJing at age 14
- youngest ever male singer to have a UK number 1 hit (April, 2000)
- won various music industry awards since then
- also recorded his song *Rise And Fall* in Punjabi
- met Nelson Mandela
- called "England's best singer" by Sir Elton John
- played many charity concerts and football matches
- received honorary Doctor of Music degree from Southampton University (2008)

Craig David was born in 1981 in Southampton, England. He has been singing and DJing ...

2 Grammar
★ had better / should / ought to

a Circle the correct words in these sentences.

a You'd **better** / should / ought do it before Mum comes home!
b You *oughtn't* / *better not* / *shouldn't* play with matches.
c You *ought not* / *better not* / *shouldn't* to let him use the internet at night.
d You *better* / *should* / *ought* talk to some of your teachers about it.
e You'd *should* / *better* / *ought* wear some smart clothes. You need to look your best!
f You *ought* / *should* / *better* to look at the advertisements in the paper.

b Match the problems below with the advice in Exercise 2a. Write the letters a–f in the boxes.

1 'My son spends all night in chat rooms.' — c
2 'I've burnt my fingers.'
3 'I want a good part-time job.'
4 'I've got a job interview tomorrow.'
5 'I don't know what career I want.'
6 'I haven't tidied up my bedroom yet.'

3 Pronunciation
★ /ɔː/ short

a There are fourteen words on this page that have the sound /ɔː/. Can you find them all? Don't repeat the same word, and don't include *for* (because this has the sound /fə/).

b ▶ CD2 T11 Listen to the fourteen words, and repeat.

4 Vocabulary

★ Jobs and work

a Complete the crossword by solving the clues with words from page 31 of the Student's Book.

Across
4. Not working all of the working week (4-4)
7. You have this if you've done the job before (10)
9. Working the complete week (4-4)
10. Leave a job (6)
11. This is your money from work (6)

Down
1. A worker for a company (8)
2. You can get them from school and university (14)
3. Without a job (10)
5. Someone who is learning the skills of a job (7)
6. Try to get a job (5)
8. The person/employer you work for (8)

4 across: PART-TIME

b Complete the two dialogues with words from the box.

> salary qualifications applied employer employees

Interviewer: Well, Ms Lane, I see you have 10 GCSEs, and six of them with an A grade. Those are very impressive _qualifications_. Why have you ¹_____ for a job with us?

Ms Lane: I think you're a very fair ²_____. You treat your ³_____ very well from what I hear. And the ⁴_____ is excellent for a first job.

> full-time part-time resigned trainee unemployed

Job Shop Officer: Are you in _full-time_ work at the moment, Alan?

Alan: No, I'm not working at all. I've been ¹_____ for the last two weeks.

Job Shop Officer: I see you ²_____ from your previous job in your first month as a ³_____. What happened?

Alan: The training programme was very poor. I wanted to find something better.

Job Shop Officer: I see. Well, we only have ⁴_____ jobs in your field at the moment – mornings, Monday to Friday, 20 hours a week. Would that interest you?

★ Fields of work

c Match the jobs 1–8 with the fields of work. Add more jobs if you can.

a public service   5
b education   _____
c entertainment   _____
d health care   _____
e IT and media   _____
f legal   _____
g finance   _____
h management   _____

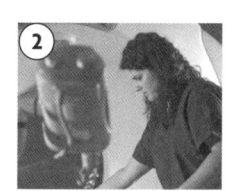

94 UNIT 4

5 Fiction in mind

a You are going to read more of *The Book of Thoughts*. Chester has discovered that the old book he found in the antique shop really does tell him what other people are thinking. But will this help him at work?

While you read the extract, choose the best word to complete the gaps.

1. a computer   b (secretary)   c manager
2. a away   b about   c around
3. a Maybe   b However   c If
4. a work   b worked   c working
5. a told   b said   c spoke

Chester walked into his office. His ¹ *secretary* was already busy typing.

'Any messages, Miss Han?' he asked her.

'Yes, Sir,' said Miss Han, 'from the Manager. He says he can't go the meeting today about the Eastern business. He wants you to take over right ² ....'

Yes!

This was the kind of opportunity he'd been waiting for. He would show them all just how good he was. This was an important piece of business. ³ .... he could make sure that everything went well he would get noticed. He would be an obvious choice for the next manager's job. If he became a manager he would be the youngest manager in the business! [...]

When he met the others Chester was confident and did his job well. He made sure that everybody knew what to do. The meeting that afternoon was sure to be a success. If, of course, the figures he had were all correct.

Just then he noticed a little smile on the face of Mr Shaw. 'What's the old man got to smile about?' thought Chester. 'He never smiles – why is he smiling now?' Then he remembered his little book.

He took it out of his pocket and hid it behind some papers. He pretended to be looking at his notes and thought of Mr Shaw. The words appeared immediately:

I'll teach that young fool a lesson. I've got some figures he doesn't know about hidden in my office. I've been ⁴ .... on this longer than he has. When he can't come up with the right figures, he'll look stupid. Then I'll produce them and save the day. He'll look like a boy trying to do a man's job. He needs to learn some respect for serious professionals like me.

Chester felt a cold sweat on the back of his neck.

'So the old man really does dislike me, after all!'

Chester wondered what all the others thought about him but had no time to consult his book.

'Thanks everybody – see you all this afternoon', Chester ⁵ .... them all. 'Enjoy your lunch.'

(from Brennan, F. (2000) 'The Book of Thoughts' in *The Fruitcake Special*, CUP: pp 56–57)

---

b Choose the correct answer: a, b, c or d.

1. Why is Chester so pleased at his secretary's news?
   a. He'll have the chance to take some time off.
   b. He'll be able to work more closely with Mr Shaw.
   c. He'll have the chance to earn his manager's respect.
   d. He'll be able to find out what his work colleagues think of him.

2. Why does Chester use the little book?
   a. To check his figures for the meeting.
   b. To read Mr Shaw's thoughts.
   c. To write what he thinks about the office employees.
   d. To hide his figures from Mr Shaw.

3. How does Chester feel at the end of the extract?
   a. cold   b. uncomfortable   c. cheerful   d. hungry

Skills in mind

6 Listen and write

a ▶CD2 T12 Listen to Chris describing a concert he saw, and complete the missing information 1–7.

b Match the underlined words and phrases a–d in the text with phrases 1–4.

1. all in all ☐
2. in conclusion ☐
3. was held ☐
4. well worth it ☐

WRITING TIP

Report writing

A report is similar to a description or review. It is normally written in a clear, semi-formal style, divided into paragraphs with headings to show what kind of information the reader will find. The report usually ends with a recommendation, which may contain your opinion.

- It helps to use headings for your paragraphs. You can then plan what you want to write, and your report will be easier to read.
- Try to learn useful words and expressions such as those underlined in the report and in Exercise 6b.
- Try to present your information as factually as you can, leaving your main opinions for the conclusion.
- In your conclusion, give a balanced assessment if possible. Be careful not to repeat what you wrote in previous paragraphs. If you are saying that you did not like something, try to find something positive to say.

Introduction

This report will describe a live event I attended recently. The event was a pop concert featuring ¹ _____ten_____ different singers and bands. Some of the money from ² _____ sales was given to charity, for people with physical and mental disabilities.

Venue and cost

The concert ᵃ <u>took place</u> at the M.E.N. Arena in Manchester. Tickets were ³ _____ , depending on where the seats were.

Atmosphere

At the beginning of the show, the sound wasn't ⁴ _____ . Later, the quality improved a lot. The lighting was very impressive. The crowd was very young; the average age was probably about ⁵ _____ .

Performances

Most of the performers played ⁶ _____ songs. There were some delays between performances. The Black Eyed Peas were the main band; they played last. I thought Lady Gaga was the best performer; her singing and dancing were excellent, and the audience responded very well.

Conclusion

ᵇ <u>To sum up</u>, the show was ⁷ _____ long, which was ᶜ <u>good value for money</u>. Not all performers were equally good, though, and perhaps it would be a good idea to cut the number of performers. This show is touring the country, and my recommendation is that, if you like just two or three of the artists, you should definitely go and see it. ᵈ <u>Overall</u>, it was an excellent evening, with something for everyone.

c Your class is doing a survey on live events that they have attended (music concerts, dance and theatre performances, craft fairs, sports, etc.). Write a report of 120–150 words about a live event you have seen, including:

- where the event was held
- the cost
- a general description
- what you liked/didn't like
- whether other people might like it
- a recommendation as to how it could be better

Unit check

1 Fill in the spaces

Complete the text with the words in the box.

> part-time   for   should   been   working   job   qualifications   experience   trainee   employee

Everybody keeps asking me what kind of .... *job* .... I want to do when I leave school. My mum doesn't think I¹ _____ apply ² _____ any jobs yet. She wants me to go to university and get some good ³ _____ so that I can be a teacher. My dad wants me to start ⁴ _____ for his bank as a(n) ⁵ _____ . He says I could do the job ⁶ _____ to get some ⁷ _____ , and go to college on my days off. I don't know if I want to be a(n) ⁸ _____ of a bank, though. I've ⁹ _____ thinking about maybe trying to sell some of my art. Decisions, decisions!

[9]

2 Choose the correct answers

Circle the correct answer: a, b or c.

1 How long have you been .... ?
 a resigning   b (unemployed)   c experienced

2 I really think you'd .... say sorry before it's too late.
 a should   b ought   c better

3 How long have you .... waiting for me?
 a just   b had   c been

4 Why don't you .... for that job? You might get it.
 a apply   b trainee   c employee

5 .... she be doing that?
 a Has   b Should   c Had

6 It looks like she .... been crying.
 a has   b just   c have

7 She's a good .... and I like working for her.
 a employee   b women   c employer

8 I didn't get the job as I don't have enough work ....
 a trainee   b experience   c qualification

9 When do you think we .... to tell them we're leaving?
 a ought   b should   c better

[8]

3 Vocabulary

Match the two parts of sentences. Write a–i in the boxes.

1 Volunteering is a good way — **g** — a apart from teaching.
2 If you don't like your job, — [ ] — b in the application form.
3 You should apply — [ ] — c in to the legal field.
4 If you like, I'll help you fill — [ ] — d you to get a good job.
5 Good qualifications will help — [ ] — e maybe you should resign.
6 There are other jobs in education — [ ] — f for a job in IT.
7 The entertainment field is more — [ ] — g to get some experience.
8 I'd rather have my own business — [ ] — h than just acting and singing.
9 Studying law is a good way — [ ] — i than be somebody's employee.

[8]

How did you do?

Total: [25]

| 😊 Very good 20 – 25 | 😐 OK 14 – 19 | ☹ Review Unit 4 again 0 – 13 |

5 Live forever!

1 Grammar
★ Future predictions

a Complete the sentences with the correct form of *(not) be likely to*.

1 'It's nice, but it **'s likely to** be really expensive.'

2 'Please write it down, because I _____ forget.'

3 'You _____ fail the exam.'

4 'He _____ play again for about six months.'

5 'I _____ pass, am I?'

6 'Perhaps we shouldn't play here – we _____ break something.'

b Complete the sentences. Use the information in the chart.

100%	will	
75%	will probably	be likely to
50%	might / might not	
25%	probably won't	not be likely to
0%	won't	

1 It / rain at the weekend. (75% + *will*)
   It will probably rain at the weekend.

2 My parents / be unhappy with my results. (100%)

3 My brother / arrive late tomorrow. (75% + *likely*)

4 The match on Saturday / be very good. (0%)

5 I / go to the cinema this evening. (50%)

6 I / pass next week's test. (75% + *likely*)

7 They / be at home tomorrow. (25% + *not likely*)

8 There / be much to eat at the party. (25% + *won't*)

9 We / visit our grandparents next weekend. (50% + *not*)

c Rewrite the sentences. Use the words in brackets.

1 The chances of my father buying me a computer are small. (likely)
   My father isn't likely to buy me a computer.

2 It's possible that I will pass the exams. (might)

3 It's possible that he won't arrive on time. (might not)

4 I'm almost sure that I'll be late. (probably)

5 There is a small chance my mother will lend me some money. (not likely)

6 I don't think that my sister will buy that car. (probably won't)

_____

7 It's very possible that they will be at the party. (likely)

_____

2 Grammar

✱ First conditional review: *if* and *unless*

a Complete the sentences with the present simple form of the verbs, or *will/won't*.

1 I ___will lend___ (lend) you the money if you ___promise___ (promise) to give it back tomorrow.

2 If she _____ (phone) me tonight, I _____ (ask) her to go out with me.

3 The door _____ (not open) unless you _____ (push) it hard.

4 Unless we _____ (leave) now, we _____ (be) late for school.

5 If he _____ (not be) careful, he _____ (hurt) himself.

6 I _____ (not come) if you _____ (not want) me to.

7 Unless you _____ (stop) talking, the teacher _____ (get) angry with you.

8 The dog _____ (not bite) you if you _____ (leave) it alone.

b Make conditional sentences with the words below.

1 you / have an accident / unless / you go more slowly
   ___You'll have an accident unless you go more slowly.___

2 If / John / invite me to the party, / I / go
   _____

3 I / beat Sally / unless / I / play badly
   _____

4 I / be very upset / if / he / lose my camera
   _____

5 Unless / you / go now, / the shops / be closed
   _____

6 If / my friend / come round, / we / play computer games
   _____

3 Grammar

✱ Time conjunctions: *if / unless / when / until / as soon as*

a Circle the correct words.

1 I'll tell you *until* / (*as soon as*) I know.

2 Mary isn't here yet so let's wait *until* / *when* she arrives.

3 I'm going to buy a new computer *when* / *unless* I have enough money.

4 You won't pass the exams *if* / *unless* you study more.

5 We'll go out *as soon as* / *unless* the weather gets better.

6 I'll stay at home *as soon as* / *until* it stops raining.

7 *When* / *Unless* we move house, I'll have my own bedroom.

8 *If* / *Until* I fail my driving test, I'll take it again.

b Complete the sentences. Use *if*, *unless*, *until* or *as soon as*.

1 She's coming home at 6.00. I'll talk to her ___as soon as___ she arrives.

2 _____ we hurry up, we'll be late for the film!

3 Dad's picking us up in the car, so we'll have to wait _____ he gets here.

4 What will you do _____ you don't pass your exams?

5 Can you do me a favour? Look after my cat _____ I get back from holiday, please.

6 I can't buy it _____ my parents lend me some money.

7 I can't talk now, I'm watching a football match – but I'll ring you _____ it finishes, OK?

8 _____ the cinema's full, don't worry – we can come back home and watch a video.

UNIT 5   99

4 Vocabulary

★ Verbs with prepositions

a Find five words in the grid to complete the phrases.

G	A	R	G	E	T	T	I	N	G
R	R	E	O	V	T	H	N	E	R
O	G	A	R	R	H	I	R	A	E
W	O	R	R	Y	I	N	G	R	V
O	I	N	A	N	N	K	O	N	I
R	V	I	S	I	K	O	I	I	S
I	W	N	K	G	I	N	N	G	I
A	R	G	U	I	N	G	G	T	N
N	Y	R	R	I	G	O	I	R	G
G	E	T	T	T	I	N	G	S	W

Common causes of stress:

1 _____ with people
2 _____ about your problems
3 _____ for exams
4 _____ about what to wear
5 _____ ready for school

b Look at the pictures. Complete the sentences with the expressions from Exercise 4a.

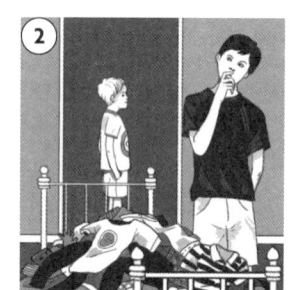

1 I hate _getting ready_ for school! I almost always forget a book or something.
2 My brother's going to a party tonight, and he's spent hours _____ .
3 I think _____ is pointless! Either you've learned the things already, or you haven't!
4 Don't sit there _____ – go and do something about them!
5 He's a really unpleasant guy – he's always _____ and fighting.

c Complete the sentences with the correct prepositions.

1 I'm a bit worried _about_ my sister.
2 My parents are thinking _____ moving to another town.
3 School ends next week, so I'm getting ready _____ the summer holidays.
4 Which exam are you revising _____ ?
5 Why are you always arguing _____ your parents?
6 What are you waiting _____ ?

5 Pronunciation

★ Weak and strong forms of prepositions

▶ **CD2 T13** Listen and repeat. Pay particular attention to the underlined words.

1 I'm looking <u>for</u> my books.
2 What are you waiting <u>for</u>?
3 Sorry – I don't want to talk <u>to</u> you.
4 Who are you writing <u>to</u>?
5 Are you looking <u>at</u> me?
6 Who are you looking <u>at</u>?

6 Vocabulary bank — Complete the cartoons with the correct prepositions.

1 "I'd like to apply __for__ the job of bank manager."

2 "My son doesn't like some of the parents I go round _____."

3 "I don't think I'll go _____ dessert, thanks."

4 "We can only hope _____ someone to find us soon."

5 "Do you think they'll have anything to talk _____?"

6 "We'll probably be able to laugh _____ it one day."

7 Study help

★ Learning and recording words in context

- It's very important to record words that you learn in a context – in other words, don't record them as words on their own.

- For example: if you learn the verb 'worry', you could record it as one word and then write a translation, e.g. 'worry = *preocuparse*'.

- But in order to use the word 'worry', you need to know and remember words that go with it – e.g. the preposition 'about'. So it's much better to write a sentence or phrase that uses the other words too, e.g. 'She never seems to worry about anything'. (You can add a translation if you think it's important and useful.)

- It's also a good idea to record your own sentences/phrases, about things which are true for you – this makes new language much more memorable.

Write sentences/phrases in your notebook (or here) which will help you remember and use these words from the unit:

argue _____

get ready _____

unless _____

as soon as _____

likely _____

Skills in mind

8 Write

a Read this advertisement in a newspaper. The advertisement requests information about four different things. What are they?

b A young man called André wrote a letter to apply for one of the jobs. Read his letter and say which of the four requests for information in the advertisement he <u>doesn't</u> respond to.

Dear Sir or Madam

I am writing to apply for a summer camp job in the UK.

I am an independent and reliable person. ¹<u>Unless I get one of the jobs,</u> I will work hard and I am sure that I will be a good employee.

I think that you need patience and a good sense of humour to work with younger children. I believe I have these qualities, but I also think that ²<u>they are likely improve</u> through this work. I think I will also learn how to deal with difficult children, and to provide discipline when it is needed.

It has always been my dream to visit Britain. I believe that my English will improve, and I am sure that I ³<u>will to learn</u> a lot of things about a different and foreign culture.

⁴<u>Thank you for consider</u> my application. I look forward to your reply.

Yours faithfully

André Le Bendit

---

c Each of the <u>underlined</u> phrases 1–4 contains a language mistake. Correct each one.

d Imagine that you want to apply for one of the summer camp jobs. Write your letter in about 120–180 words. (Don't count the opening and your name.)

SUMMER CAMPS UK

Wanted: young people to work on a holiday camp for 10- to 13-year-old children in the UK for a period of three months. Various locations in the country. The work includes organising entertainment for the children and general cleaning duties.

If you are interested in this position, write and tell us:

- why you think you are suitable for the post
- about your level of English (exams you have passed / hope to pass in the future)
- what you think you will gain from working with younger children
- what you think you will gain or learn from being in the UK for three months

Write to PO Box 788, Cheltenham, UK before April 30 this year.

WRITING TIP

Writing a letter for an exam

When you write a letter, especially for a test or an examination, remember that you should always:

- Read the task carefully and do exactly what it asks you to do. In this example, you need to read the advertisement carefully and make sure that you provide all the information that the advertisement asks for. If you miss out important information, you will lose a lot of marks.

- Check your own writing carefully when you have finished. Check for grammar mistakes and for any spelling mistakes. In exams especially, it is easy to make small mistakes under pressure. Give yourself time at the end to check.

- Check your text, if there is a word limit, to make sure that you have used about the required number of words. If you don't write enough words, you will lose marks. If you write far too many, the examiner won't mark much beyond the word limit.

Unit check

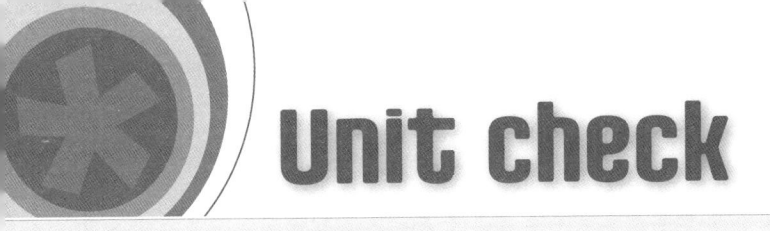

1 Fill in the spaces

Complete the text with the words in the box.

| until | If | unless | likely | might | probably | for | about | ~~when~~ | with |

I'm not very sure what to do ……*when*…… I leave school. ¹…………… I do well in my exams, I ²…………… go to university, but I ³…………… won't get good enough grades – I haven't revised ⁴…………… the exams very much at all. So I think that perhaps I'll get a job, save some money and then travel a bit, ⁵…………… I haven't got any money left. When I told my parents about that, they weren't very happy and they argued ⁶…………… me for a long time. They said they were worried ⁷…………… me, and they didn't want me to go. And I don't think they're ⁸…………… to change their minds. So, ⁹…………… I can think of something else, I still won't know what to do when I leave school!

[9]

2 Choose the correct answers

Circle the correct answer: a, b or c.

1 …………… the weather's nice this weekend, we can have a picnic.
  a (If) b When c As soon as

2 Why do you always argue …………… me?
  a to b at c with

3 I can't come out tonight – I'm revising …………… my exams.
  a for b about c to

4 I don't want to leave – I want to stay …………… the film finishes.
  a until b if c when

5 I'll phone you as soon as I …………… anything.
  a am hearing b will hear c hear

6 I can't stand her – she only ever thinks …………… herself.
  a for b about c with

7 They won't know …………… you don't tell them.
  a unless b when c if

8 Mike's upstairs – he's …………… ready for tonight's party.
  a going b getting c being

9 You won't pass the test …………… you study hard.
  a as soon as b when c unless

[8]

3 Vocabulary

Circle the correct words.

1 What a cool camera! We're going to have some fun (with) / for it.

2 I had a great chat by / with my dad last night. He's not as old as I thought!

3 If / When you had loads of money, what would you do?

4 Let's pray for / with good weather this weekend for the party.

5 I dreamed about / by you last night. It was a really weird dream.

6 I can't go out tonight. I've got to revise about / for my exams.

7 We're in a hurry. We've got to leave until / as soon as we've had lunch.

8 It took him hours to get ready for / by the party. Was it worth it?

9 I won't help you unless / if you say 'sorry' for being mean to me this morning.

[8]

How did you do?

Total: [25]

| 😊 Very good 20 – 25 | 😐 OK 14 – 19 | ☹ Review Unit 5 again 0 – 13 |

UNIT 5   103

6 Reality TV

1 Grammar

★ make / let / be allowed to

a Put the words in the correct order to make sentences.

1 a noise / aren't / to / You / make / allowed
   You aren't allowed to make a noise.

2 travellers / to / The / allowed / enter / weren't / the country
   _____

3 parents / play outside / let / Our / never / us
   _____

4 us / The / didn't / leave / early / let / teacher
   _____

5 mobile / made / switch off / our / They / us / phones
   _____

6 make / Do / before / your parents / bed / you / to / go / 10 o'clock?
   _____

b Look at the signs. Write sentences with *(not) allowed to*.

1 *You aren't allowed to cycle/ride your bike here.*

2 _____

3 _____

4 _____

5 _____

6 _____ but _____

c Rewrite the sentences. Use the words in brackets.

1 We don't have permission to go into that room. (allow)
   We *aren't allowed to go into that room.*

2 The teacher told us to stay longer at school yesterday. (make)
   The teacher _____ .

3 I don't allow my sister to borrow my things. (let)
   I _____ .

4 My father didn't give me permission to borrow his car. (let)
   My father _____ .

5 You can't smoke here. (allow)
   You _____ .

6 My mum says I have to pay for my own mobile phone. (make)
   My mum _____ .

2 Vocabulary

✱ Television

a Match the words with the definitions. Write 1–8 in the boxes.

> 1 episode 2 series 3 celebrities 4 viewing figures 5 audience
> 6 sitcoms 7 presenter 8 viewer 9 contestant 10 quiz show

a A group of programmes about the same subject. **2**
b Comedy programmes about the lives of ordinary people. ☐
c A person who takes part in a 10. ☐
d One part of a 2. ☐
e The person who presents a programme. ☐
f People who watch a TV programme in the studio. ☐
g The number of people who watch a programme. ☐
h A programme where people answer questions. ☐
i A person who is watching a TV programme at home (not in the studio). ☐
j Well-known people on television (or in films). ☐

b Complete the sentences with the correct form of the words at the end of each line.

Yesterday evening I watched a __wonderful__ new quiz show on TV.   WONDER
There are four ¹_____, who have to answer really hard   CONTEST
questions that the ²_____ asks them. If they don't know the answer   PRESENT
to a question, they are ³_____ to phone home and get some help.   ALLOW
And sometimes the ⁴_____ at home can phone the programme and   VIEW
ask questions too. The ⁵_____ gets a prize of a new car! I think   WIN
it's going to be a very ⁶_____ show.   SUCCESS

3 Pronunciation

✱ /aʊ/ allowed

a ▶ CD2 T14 Tick (✔) the words which have the /aʊ/ sound in them. Then listen, check and repeat.

1 how ✔
2 know ☐
3 now ☐
4 mouse ☐
5 loud ☐
6 shout ☐
7 slow ☐
8 house ☐
9 found ☐
10 snow ☐

b ▶ CD2 T15 Listen and repeat.

1 How do you know which house it is?
2 I found a mouse in the snow.
3 We heard a loud shout.
4 There was a mouse running loudly round the house.

4 Grammar

✱ Modal verbs of obligation, prohibition and permission

a Complete the sentences with the words in the box.

> have to go   mustn't go   can't bring
> don't have to stay   can stay   ~~must bring~~

1 'OK, tomorrow afternoon is sports, so you __must bring__ your sports clothes, OK?'
2 'Great! My dad says I _____ out as late as I want to.'
3 'Sorry, I'm really late for my meeting. I _____ now.'
4 'Are you bored? Well, look – you _____ here if you don't want to.'
5 'Hey, Alex, that's the girls' toilet, you _____ in there!'
6 'Sorry, you _____ your dog into the library. No animals are allowed in here.'

UNIT 6   105

b Look at the pictures. What are the people saying? Complete the sentences.

1 'We _can't_ leave through here.'
2 'You _____ feed the animals!' 
3 'You _____ open it now if you want.' 
4 'We _____ show something to prove we're 18.'  
5 'I _____ clear up this mess!' 
6 'Great! I _____ wear a suit and tie!' 

5 Vocabulary
★ Extreme adjectives and modifiers

a Complete the sentences with the words in the box.

> fantastic enormous awful boiling exhausted
> hilarious ~~tiny~~ starving freezing fascinating

1 A: My dog is so small and cute!   B: Small? She's _tiny_!
2 A: Was it hot in Australia?   B: Yes it was! In fact, it was _____.
3 A: This is a good song.   B: Yes, it's _____.
4 A: Is it cold outside?   B: It's _____.
5 A: Is her new flat big?   B: It certainly is. In fact, it's _____.
6 A: Are you still feeling bad?   B: Yes, I feel really _____.
7 A: He's so funny!   B: I know. He's _____.
8 A: What an interesting story!   B: Yes, it was _____.
9 A: Are you hungry?   B: I'm _____!
10 A: I think they're tired.   B: Tired? They're _____!

b **Vocabulary bank** Respond to the questions with *Yes* and an adjective from the word bank. Sometimes more than one answer is possible.

1 The pizza was bad, wasn't it?
   Yes, it was disgusting.
2 Were you scared by that thunder?
   _____
3 Was the band really loud?
   _____
4 Is the soup tasty?
   _____
5 Were you happy with your present?
   _____
6 Are you excited about Disneyland?
   _____
7 Is it really bad news?
   _____

6 Vocabulary
★ Making new friends

Replace the underlined words with phrasal verbs from the box.

> feel left out   bond with   fit in
> join in

1 Karen's playing with her new puppy. She's trying to make a close connection with it.
   _____
2 What's wrong with you, Sam? Don't you want to be part of the game?
   _____
3 I'm not going out with Harry and his friends any more. I just don't feel like I belong.
   _____
4 Here's a present for you, Tom. I don't want you to think you're not being included.
   _____

106 UNIT 6

7 Culture in mind

a Read the text about this song. Some of the lines of the text have an extra, unnecessary word. Write the word at the end of the line. If the line is correct, tick it.

Somebody's Watching Me by Rockwell

The song *Somebody's Watching Me* it was recorded by a singer called	1 _it_
Rockwell. Rockwell was in fact a man called Kennedy Gordy, who was	2 ✓
the son of Berry Gordy, the man who he started Motown Records.	3
Gordy changed his the name because he wanted to make records, but he	4
also did wanted to be recognised for his talent. He signed with Motown	5
as a solo artist without his father's knowledge, and took his name from his	6
high school band. Rockwell's sister, Hazel, was married to the Jermaine Jackson,	7
Michael Jackson's brother, and that's why Rockwell was able to can get Michael	8
and Jermaine to sing with on the recording. The song was a big hit and went	9
to number 2 in the charts in 1984. Rockwell then revealed his true identity.	10
But he didn't have much more success and his next album didn't sell well not at all.	11

b Read the text again. Mark the statements *T* (true), *F* (false) or *N* (no information).

1 Rockwell's real name was Berry Gordy. _F_
2 Motown Records started in Detroit, USA.
3 Berry Gordy knew that his son had signed with Motown.
4 Jermaine Jackson was Rockwell's brother-in-law.
5 *Somebody's Watching Me* was a successful single.
6 Rockwell's next album sold less than ten thousand copies.

c ▶ CD2 T16 Listen to Dave telling a friend about the video for *Somebody's Watching Me*. Put the pictures in the correct order. Write numbers 1–6 in the boxes.

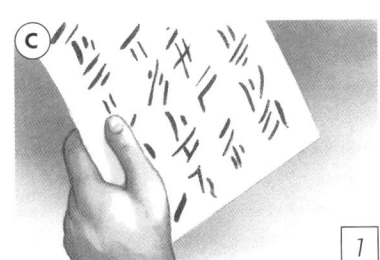

A
B
C [1]
D
E
F

d Here are three lines from the song. Which pictures are they related to?

1 But maybe showers remind me of *Psycho* too much.
2 Well, can the people on TV see me or am I just paranoid?
3 Well, is the mailman watching me?

Skills in mind

8 Write

a Paul and Sandra had to write articles for their school magazine. Do not write anything yet, but read what they had to do:

> **Write an article about your favourite television programme. Write about:**
> - the kind of programme it is, and how often it is on TV
> - who the people in the programme are
> - what the programme is about
> - what you especially like in the programme and why
> - who you would recommend it to
>
> **Write between 120 and 150 words.**

b Read Paul and Sandra's answers. Complete the sentences with the words from the box.

> been going   very believable
> no matter   ~~on the market~~
> a good reason

c Which of the two articles do you think is better? Why?

d Write an article for your school magazine. Use the same task as Paul and Sandra's.

My favourite programme is *Top Gear*. It's a programme about cars, and I love it because I'm a car freak but also because the presenters are really funny, especially Jeremy Clarkson.

They look at new cars that are ¹ <u>on the market</u> , and sometimes they're really critical (for example, once Jeremy Clarkson said a car was very cheap, and there was ² _____ – it was awful!).

There are four presenters – the other three are Richard Hammond, James May and The Stig. It's on once a week, usually at about 8.00 in the evening.   (Paul – 89 words)

My favourite programme is a soap opera on the BBC called *EastEnders*. It's on twice a week, on Tuesday and Thursday evenings, for half an hour each time. It's a story about the lives of people who live in a place called Albert Square, in the east of London. It started in 1985, so the programme's ³ _____ for about twenty years now!

The reason I like *EastEnders* is that the characters are really interesting and you get into their lives. There's a good range of characters, and real things happen to them – illness, divorce, marriage, arguments and so on – so it's ⁴ _____ . The acting is excellent, too. I think that anyone who enjoys well-written and well-acted soap operas would love *EastEnders*. There's something in it for everyone, ⁵ _____ how old they are or whether they're a boy or a girl.
(Sandra – 145 words)

WRITING TIP

Organising a writing task

When you are given a writing task, make sure you follow the order of things you are asked to do. This will help you organise your writing.

Look at Paul's article, for example. Here is what he talks about, in this order:

a the name of the programme
b what it's about
c one of the presenters
d what they do on the programme
e the presenters (again)
f when the programme is on

Does Paul write about all the topics he is asked to write about?

Compare Paul's answer to Sandra's. Check:

a what the task asks for
b the information Sandra includes in her answer and the order in which she presents it

---

108   UNIT 6

Unit check

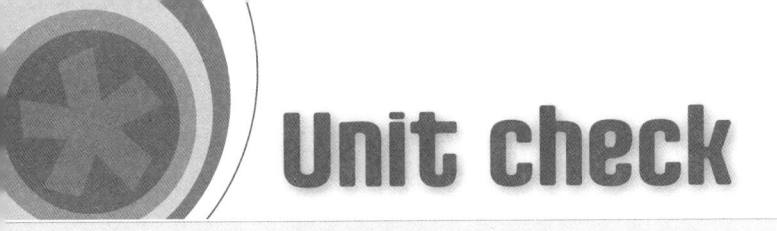

1 Fill in the spaces

Complete the text with the words in the box.

| fun | winner | presenter | contestants | freezing | ~~episodes~~ | had | allowed | made | enormous |

I'll always remember one of the __episodes__ of *Endurance*, the Japanese game show. There were six ¹_____, and they were taken to Holland in the middle of winter. They were ²_____ to take off almost all their clothes and they ³_____ to stand outside in the ⁴_____ weather. Then the ⁵_____ told them to drink as much water as they possibly could. And they did – they all drank ⁶_____ amounts of water! But that wasn't the competition. When they finished drinking, the presenter told them that they weren't ⁷_____ to go to the toilet! The ⁸_____ was the last person to go to the toilet. The presenter made ⁹_____ of them too – it was hilarious!

☐ 9

2 Choose the correct answers

Circle the correct answer: a, b or c.

1 The _____ in the studio enjoyed the programme a lot.
   a viewing   b (audience)   c ratings

2 We don't like wearing a uniform, but the school _____ us wear one.
   a makes   b lets   c allowed

3 This soap opera has the highest _____ of any TV programme in history!
   a viewers   b viewing figures   c contestants

4 The water in the shower was very cold – in fact, it was really _____ !
   a starving   b boiling   c freezing

5 It's a holiday today, so we _____ go to school.
   a don't have to   b must   c have to

6 I watched the first six _____ of the series, but then I got bored.
   a ratings   b celebrities   c episodes

7 One day I want to be a _____ in a quiz show – I'm sure I'd win!
   a presenter   b viewer   c contestant

8 A few minutes ago, I was hungry – but now I'm absolutely _____ !
   a tiny   b starving   c exhausted

9 My school doesn't _____ us to stay inside at break time.
   a let   b make   c allow

☐ 8

3 Vocabulary

Replace the underlined words so that the sentences make sense.

1 That film was absolutely <u>boring</u>. I laughed all the way through it. __hilarious__

2 Come over and <u>bond</u> in the fun. _____

3 The forest fire was really <u>terrified</u>. _____

4 I'm really <u>excited</u>. I could go to sleep right now. _____

5 Your handwriting is so <u>deafening</u> I can't read it. _____

6 I don't <u>feel comfortable</u> here. I'm so different from everyone else. _____

7 That's a(n) <u>absolutely</u> good idea. _____

8 He presented that wildlife <u>sitcom</u>, but I can't remember his name. _____

9 She's an absolutely <u>disgusting</u> singer. I think she's my favourite. _____

☐ 8

How did you do?

Total: ☐ 25

| 😊 Very good 20 – 25 | 😐 OK 14 – 19 | ☹ Review Unit 6 again 0 – 13 |

7 Survival

1 Grammar
✱ Present passive and past passive review

a Circle the correct answer: a, b, c or d.

1 Squash is a popular sport that .... indoors.
   a plays   b (is played)   c played   d was played

2 President John Kennedy .... in Dallas in November 1963.
   a kills   b is killed   c killed   d was killed

3 Many Japanese people .... sushi and sashimi.
   a eat   b are eaten   c ate   d were eaten

4 Many animals .... for scientific experiments in the past.
   a use   b are used   c used   d were used

5 Spanish .... by a lot of people in the USA.
   a speaks   b is spoken   c spoke   d was spoken

6 Honda is a company that .... cars.
   a makes   b is made   c made   d was made

b Write sentences using the present simple or past simple passive.

1 The World Trade Centre / destroy / on 11 September 2001
   The World Trade Centre was destroyed on 11 September 2001.

2 A language called Hindi / speak / in many parts of India ....

3 The 2008 Olympic Games / hold / in Beijing ....

4 Boeing 747 planes / call / Jumbos ....

5 Most American films / make / in Hollywood ....

6 The 2006 football World Cup / win / by Italy ....

7 John Lennon / kill / in December 1980 ....

8 The Titanic / sink / by an iceberg ....

9 Gorillas / find / in forests in Africa ....

10 Buildings / design / by architects ....

2 Grammar
✱ Causative *have* (have something done)

a Look at the signs. Write sentences about what you can have done at each place.

1 You can *have your pizza delivered.*

2 You can have your ....

3 You can ....

4 You ....

5 You ....

6 ....

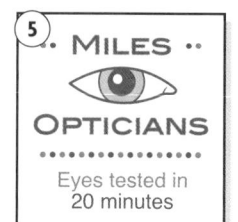

1 **pizza Home** — We deliver pizzas *fast*

2 **Photo Express** — BRING YOUR FILMS HERE — We develop in 30 minutes!

3 **Ring & Things** — We can pierce your ears in no time at all!

4 **Hard and Soft** — Let us repair your computer

5 **MILES OPTICIANS** — Eyes tested in 20 minutes

6 **Clean & Go** — We dry-clean clothes in only 12 hours

110 UNIT 7

b ▶CD2 T17 Look at the pictures and write the sentences. Choose words from the box. Then listen and check.

photograph ~~test~~ computer repair car take ~~eyes~~ build garage deliver

1 She *'s having her eyes tested.*   2 They _____.   3 He _____.

4 She _____.   5 They _____.

3 Pronunciation
★ Stress pattern in *have something done*

a ▶CD2 T17 Listen again to the sentences in Exercise 2b. Mark the stressed words.

b ▶CD2 T17 Listen again and repeat the sentences.

4 Vocabulary
★ *make* and *do*

a Match the two parts of the sentences. Write a–h in the boxes.

1 Eat fruit! It'll do — *d*
2 I dropped some paint on the floor – it made
3 It's not nice to make
4 You can do it if you make
5 She was very funny but I did
6 I don't want to invite Greg. He always makes
7 When he sold his flat he made
8 Why do some people smoke? It doesn't make

a sense to me!
b fun of other people.
c a real mess.
d you some good.
e a lot of money.
f my best not to laugh at her.
g trouble at parties.
h an effort.

b Complete the sentences with the correct form of *make* or *do*.

1 Don't just sit there! *Do* something!
2 I took the medicine the doctor gave me and it _____ me a lot of good.
3 I've read this page three times – and it still _____ (not) sense to me!
4 I've got a faster computer now, and it _____ a big difference.
5 Yesterday's exam was hard! But I _____ my best.
6 There was a group of boys trying to _____ trouble at the match.
7 I think I _____ a mess of the interview. I didn't know what to say.
8 I'm going to get a job and _____ some money.

UNIT 7 111

c **Vocabulary bank** Circle the correct words.

1 We've got to clean the whole house, so let's make a *start / room* right away.
2 I'm interested in the bike you've got for sale. I'd like to make you *a price / an offer*.
3 If you want a sofa in your room, you're going to have to take something out to make *spare / room* for it.
4 Mum, we want to make a *question / request*: can we go for a picnic at the weekend, please?
5 Paul, your father and I need to talk to you. Can you make some *room / time* to sit down with us later today?
6 Sabrina's just got a job as a fashion designer. What a great way to make a *living / job*!
7 Please go back and make *definite / sure* that you locked the front door.
8 The council are planning to knock down some houses to make *way / route* for a new motorway.

5 Grammar

★ Present perfect passive

a Complete the sentences with the words in the box.

> have been killed   has been made
> have been sold   have been made
> haven't been invited   ~~has been built~~

1 A new library _has been built_ in our town.
2 Their new CD only came out last week, but thousands of copies _____ already!
3 There's been an earthquake in our country and a lot of people _____ .
4 Many animals _____ extinct in the last twenty years.
5 They're having a party tomorrow evening – but we _____ !
6 A big effort _____ recently to keep the town clean.

b What has happened in each picture? Complete the sentences with the present perfect passive form of the verbs.

1 The woman _has been robbed_ (rob).
2 Three houses _____ (knock down).
3 Their pizzas _____ (not deliver) yet.
4 The bank robbers _____ (catch).
5 That car _____ (not clean) for weeks!
6 The fire _____ (put out).

c Rewrite the sentences to make them passive.

1 A man from Liverpool has won the £10-million pound jackpot.
   The £10-million pound jackpot has been won by a man in Liverpool.
2 Messi scored the winning goal.
   The winning goal _____ .
3 A professional decorated our house.
   Our house _____ .
4 They didn't deliver our passports to us in time.
   Our passports _____ .
5 Mr Brown deals with all complaints.
   All complaints _____ .
6 Mary always cut my hair.
   I _____ .

6 Grammar

✱ Future passive

a Look at the poster. What will be done if they are elected? Complete the sentences.

1 New schools _will be built_ .
2 Trees and parks _____ .
3 Taxes _____ .
4 Food _____ to poor families.
5 More policemen _____ on the streets.
6 Hospitals _____ .
7 New companies _____ .
8 Pollution _____ .

VOTE FOR US!

We will …
- build new schools!
- protect trees and parks!
- NOT increase taxes!
- give food to poor families!
- put more policemen on the streets!
- NOT close hospitals!
- help new companies!
- reduce pollution!

b Complete the sentences/questions. Use the future passive form of the verbs.

1 A new swimming pool _will be built_ (build) in our town next year.
2 It _____ (not finish) until next October.
3 _____ the water _____ (heat)?
4 All the swimmers _____ (supervise) by lifeguards.
5 Children under ten _____ (not allow) to swim without an adult.
6 _____ people who can't swim _____ (give) lessons?

7 Everyday English

a Complete the expressions with the words in the box.

~~mean~~ Any How More all earth

1 I _mean_
2 What on _____ (are you doing)?
3 _____ chance (you could help me)?
4 after _____
5 _____ come (you're late)?
6 _____ or less

b Complete the dialogues with the expressions in Exercise 7a.

1 A: I got the last question wrong.
   B: But it was so easy! _____ you didn't know the answer?

2 A: Like my new coat? It cost me €200!
   B: €200?? That's incredibly expensive! _____ are you doing, buying things like that?

3 A: Have you finished that book?
   B: _____ – I've just got the last ten pages to read.

4 A: Hi, David. What's the matter?
   B: Hi, Mr Jones. The thing is, I missed my bus. _____ you could take me to school?

5 A: You made a complete mess of everything!
   B: Oh, come on. That's not fair. _____ , I did my best.

6 A: He won't lend me his MP4 player! I don't understand why not.
   B: Well, maybe he's using it. And it's his MP4 player, _____ .

UNIT 7   113

Skills in mind

8 Listen

▶ CD2 T18 Listen to five short recordings. For each one, circle the correct answer: a, b or c.

1 Listen to a teacher who is talking to a group of students about a bus. What time will the bus leave?
   a 8.15
   b 8.30
   c 8.50

2 Listen to a teacher talking to a girl, Sally, about her results. What does the Maths teacher think about Sally's results?
   a She's very happy with Sally's progress.
   b She thinks that Sally could make more progress.
   c She's very angry that Sally hasn't made progress.

3 Mike is talking to Andy. What is different about Andy?
   a He's had his hair cut.
   b He's had his arm tattooed.
   c He's had his ear pierced.

4 A news announcer is talking about an earthquake. How many people have been killed?
   a About four thousand.
   b About four hundred.
   c About fourteen thousand.

5 Listen to a phone conversation – a woman is ordering a pizza. How much will she have to pay for the pizza?
   a £6.25 plus 30p for delivery.
   b £6.25 if she wants the pizza in the next 30 minutes.
   c Nothing if the pizza is not delivered within 30 minutes.

LISTENING TIP

How to answer multiple choice questions

- Read all the choices carefully and make sure you understand them. What do you have to listen for? For example, in number 1 you have to listen for a time.

- Remember that you will need to listen to the whole section before you choose your answer. Never write down the first thing you hear. For example, in number 1, the woman tells the students to be back at the bus at 8.15, but that isn't when the bus will leave. She then goes on to say it will leave 'at half past'. So, what time does the bus leave?

- Remember that you can usually hear the recording twice. Use the second listening either to check your answer, or to help you think about the correct answer.

Unit check

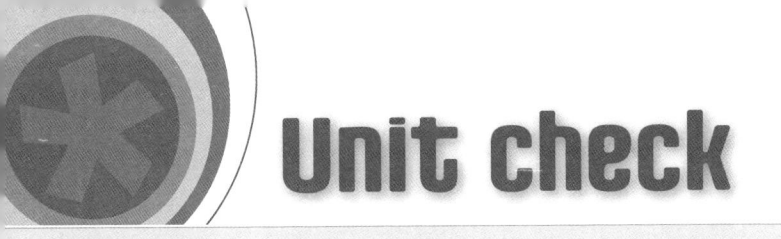

1 Fill in the spaces

Complete the text with the words in the box.

| were | was | have | had | ~~went~~ | developed |
| made | made | taken | effort | | |

Last year I needed a new passport, so I ...went... to a photo shop in town and had my photograph
¹.................. . When I went back two days later to collect the photo, I looked at it and thought it
².................. awful! The colour was strange, and I was sure it hadn't been ³.................. properly, so I
complained to the man in the shop. I said: 'You've ⁴.................. a mess of this!', but he ⁵.................. fun
of me. The manager asked me if I wanted to ⁶.................. my photo taken again. I wasn't very happy, but
I said OK, sat down and made a big ⁷.................. to smile. This time I ⁸.................. three photos taken,
but when I saw them they ⁹.................. worse than the first one because I looked so angry!

☐ 9

2 Choose the correct answers

Circle the correct answer: a, b or c.

1. Work hard and you'll .... money.
   a do   b (make)   c have

2. I need to throw some old clothes away, to make .... for the new ones.
   a room   b a mess   c an effort

3. My dad's car broke down, so he had to .... it repaired.
   a have   b do   c make

4. If you pronounce a language well, it makes a big .... for other people.
   a mess   b difference   c progress

5. A prehistoric man .... last year.
   a was found   b find   c is found

6. She went to the hairdresser's to ....
   a cut her hair   b have cut her hair
   c have her hair cut

7. Eating fruit can do you a lot of ....
   a best   b good   c better

8. Since last year, a lot of new roads ....
   a have been built   b were built   c have built

9. The government says that next year, taxes will ....
   a reduce   b be reduced   c have reduced

☐ 8

3 Vocabulary

Complete the dialogue. Write one word in each space.

Pam: Hey, Lucy, have you heard that they want to knock down the swimming pool to make ...way... for a shopping centre?

Lucy: No way! Well, I think we should all make a big ¹.................. to stop them! I'm fed up with the planners making a ².................. of our town.

Pam: I agree! I'll do my ³.................. to get some of our friends involved. Like Gerry.

Lucy: There's no point in asking Gerry. He'll just make ⁴.................. of what we're trying to do. He always laughs at us anyway.

Pam: I don't care. We're going to try to ⁵.................. some good in this town. If he wants to ⁶.................. trouble, or tease us about it, that's up to him.

Lucy: OK, well first of all let's talk to our parents and see what ideas they've got.

Pam: Yes, that makes ⁷.................. . They always have good ideas. So come on – let's make a ⁸.................. !

☐ 8

How did you do?

Total: ☐ 25

| 😊 Very good 20 – 25 | 😐 OK 14 – 19 | ☹ Review Unit 7 again 0 – 13 |

UNIT 7

8 Good and evil

1 Grammar
★ Gerunds and infinitives

a Find and (circle) seven verbs that are followed by a gerund (→←) and seven verbs that are followed by the infinitive. (↓↑)

W	T	R	E	N	J	O	Y	E	E
P	N	O	U	X	G	F	L	P	S
R	A	W	F	I	O	F	O	V	O
O	W	T	S	E	T	E	D	X	O
M	I	N	D	E	E	R	R	J	H
I	M	A	G	I	N	E	O	L	C
S	U	G	G	E	S	T	F	E	H
E	K	I	L	L	E	E	F	A	O
P	S	E	S	I	T	C	A	R	P
O	A	E	V	I	L	O	S	N	E

b Complete the sentences with the gerund or infinitive form of the verbs. Then look at page 57 of the Student's Book to check your answers.

1 Jane can't stand ……*living*…… (live) with her evil aunt.

2 Jane later decides ……………… (leave) her life teaching at the school.

3 Count Dracula wants ……………… (buy) a house near London.

4 Why must the Count avoid ……………… (see) him during the day?

5 Some of the younger children imagine ……………… (be) chased by a strange beast.

6 Jack promises ……………… (kill) the beast.

7 Bilbo Baggins enjoys ……………… (live) an ordinary life.

8 Gollum offers ……………… (let) him go free if he can solve a riddle.

c Complete the text with the correct form of the verbs in the box.

> write   help   read   ~~smoke~~   help   fight
> kill   play

Everyone knows about Sherlock Holmes, the famous Victorian detective, who enjoyed ……*smoking*…… his pipe and practised [1]……………… his violin while he thought about his latest case. Not so many people are familiar with his enemy, Professor Moriarty. Whereas Holmes promised [2]……………… evil, Moriarty chose [3]……………… it. In fact, Moriarty offered [4]……………… all the criminals in London.

When Holmes' creator, Sir Arthur Conan Doyle, didn't feel like [5]……………… any more detective stories, he decided [6]……………… both characters. In a famous scene from *The Final Problem* (1893), Moriarty and Holmes fell to their deaths while fighting on top of the Reichenbach waterfalls in Switzerland.

However, under pressure from his readers who missed [7]……………… about their favourite detective, Conan Doyle brought Holmes back to life for 1903's *The Adventure of the Empty House*. So did Moriarty really die? Only one man knows.

d Put the words in the correct order to make sentences.

1. friends / I / really / with / enjoy / time / spending / my

   I really enjoy spending time with my friends.

2. again / see / I / to / you / want / soon

   _____

3. help / school / to / My / offered / me / after / teacher

   _____

4. called / being / detests / Timothy / He

   _____

5. imagine / with / I / getting / angry / can't / him

   _____

6. to / more / to / have / patient / learn / You'll / be

   _____

e Complete the sentences with verbs from box A and box B in the correct forms.

Box A	Box B
feel like miss practise afford avoid mind ~~offer~~ promise	give go speak buy live get up study ~~lend~~

1. Dad __offered__ __to lend__ me his car for the weekend. Where shall we go?
2. I really don't _____ _____ to school today. I want to stay in bed all day!
3. I can't _____ _____ a new computer. I've only saved €300.
4. This city's so noisy. I really _____ _____ by the sea.
5. She _____ _____ me her answer tomorrow. I hope she says 'yes'.
6. I need someone _____ _____ French with. I've got my oral test next week.
7. I don't _____ _____ early but I prefer to sleep in at weekends.
8. I always _____ _____ the night before a test.

2 Vocabulary

★ Noun suffixes

a Write the noun forms of the words in the box in the correct columns.

kind   popular   ~~relax~~   protect   prefer   probable   react
enjoy   prepare   imagine   agree   differ   entertain   possible

-ation	-ence	-ment	-ness	-ion	-ity
relaxation					

b Complete the text with the correct form of the words.

James Bond's ¹ *popularity* is as big as it has ever been.   POPULAR
Today's audiences continue to ² _____ 007, half a century   ENJOYMENT
after his first appearance in 1962's *Dr No*.
Bond still offers the world ³ _____ from villains   PROTECT
by using his ⁴ _____ .   IMAGINE
Young or old, male or female, audiences all ⁵ _____   AGREEMENT
that Bond films are still great ⁶ _____ .   ENTERTAIN

C **Vocabulary bank** Complete the sentences with the correct form of the words.

1 I love films with lots of ____action____ . (act)
2 That's a bad cut. I think you might need hospital _____ . (treat)
3 I wonder what kind of _____ we'll get this time. (punish)
4 What a great _____ ! Let's go right now. (suggest)
5 Will I get an _____ to your party? (invite)
6 Looking directly at the sun can cause _____ . (blind)
7 You need a lot of _____ to write a good sitcom. (create)
8 Let me show you this great job _____ . (advertise)
9 It's _____ to think you can pass the exams without studying. (mad)

3 Pronunciation

✱ Word stress

a ▶ CD2 T19 Listen and underline the stressed syllables. In which pairs of words does the stress change?

1 prepare   preparation
2 prefer   preference
3 enjoy   enjoyment
4 lazy   laziness
5 protect   protection
6 popular   popularity

b Practise saying each pair of words.

4 Grammar

✱ Verbs with gerunds or infinitives

a Match the sentences with the pictures. Write A–D in the boxes.

1 I stopped to have a look at the map. [B]
2 I remember posting the letter. [ ]
3 I remembered to post the letter. [ ]
4 I stopped looking at the map. [ ]

b Match the questions and the answers.

1 Did you remember to phone Jane?
2 Don't you remember telling that joke before?
3 Why are you so late?
4 Do you want a hamburger?
5 When are you going to stop playing that game?

a No thanks, I've stopped eating meat.
b I'm on the last level. Nearly done!
c No, I'll give her a call now.
d I stopped to buy you some flowers.
e Oh, I'm sorry. Well, it's still funny.

c (Circle) the correct words. Sometimes there is more than one possibility.

1 It's started *to snow* / *snowing*. Snowball fights!
2 I remember *to see* / *seeing* that girl at Rachel's party. Who is she?
3 I hate *to watch* / *watching* romantic films.
4 I stopped *to eat* / *eating* chicken years ago.
5 I stopped *to buy* / *buying* a CD on my way home.
6 She loves *to go* / *going* to the cinema on Saturday afternoons.
7 Did you remember *to tell* / *telling* Owen where we're meeting tonight?
8 They began *to work* / *working* on the road at 6am. Can you believe it?

5 Fiction in mind

a Read more from *The Water of Wanting* by Frank Brennan. What happened to the two sets of laboratory mice? What do you think the water contains?

Jean Pascal put a small drop of clear liquid into the drinking water of his mice.

¹ _____ But Jean soon noticed that when there was liquid in the water, they came back to drink it more than usual. They couldn't have been thirsty any more, but they drank. He needed to check this carefully.

Jean was now a brilliant chemist. He worked in Montreal, Canada, for a large chemical company. His company made a lot of different chemicals – including chemicals for food, which are often called additives. Additives give food a different colour or flavour or even make it last longer. ² _____

The mice kept coming back for more water. Their stomachs were already completely full of liquid, but they still wanted to drink more. They just couldn't get enough water which had Jean's additive in it. They didn't want to eat any food at all. ³ _____ And, amazingly, they were still trying to reach the water when they died.

He cut the amount of WOW that he added to his mice's water by half. ⁴ _____ Then he added much smaller amounts of WOW: the mice drank less, but they still came back for little drinks of water all the time. These little drinks were still far more than the mice needed. It was as if they had become addicted to water. They weren't interested in anything else. They didn't even want food. This time they didn't die of too much water. They all died of hunger.

(from Brennan, F. (2009) 'Water of Wanting' in *Tasty Tales*, CUP: pp 4–6)

b Read the extract again and put one of the following sentences in each space. There is one sentence you won't need.

- A Food companies pay a lot of money for additives which work well.
- B Normally, the mice drank only when they were thirsty.
- C Soon they died because their tiny bodies were too full of water.
- E It was big and expensive and it exploded in his face.
- F The results were the same.

c Choose the correct way to complete the statements, according to the text.

1. In his first experiment, Jean observed that
   a the mice were eating more than usual.
   b the liquid affected the mice's thirst.
   c the mice died almost immediately.
   d he had put too much liquid into the water.

2. Food additives
   a can keep food fresh for longer.
   b are mostly manufactured in Canada.
   c are natural parts of most food.
   d do not change the way something tastes.

3. The first group of mice
   a drank all the water at once.
   b finally became satisfied and stopped drinking.
   c ate too much and couldn't drink any more water.
   d didn't realise the water was killing them.

4. In the second experiment,
   a the WOW concentration was doubled.
   b the mice still drank more than was necessary.
   c the mice drank even more than before.
   d the mice died the same way as in the first experiment.

Skills in mind

6 Listen

a ▶ CD2 T20 You will hear part of an interview with a film critic about how monsters have changed in films. Listen and tick (✔) the characters he mentions.

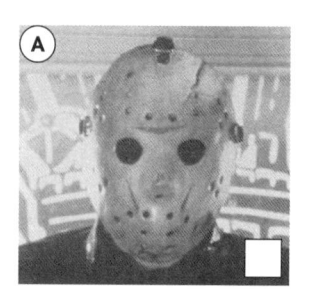

A
Friday 13th: Jason

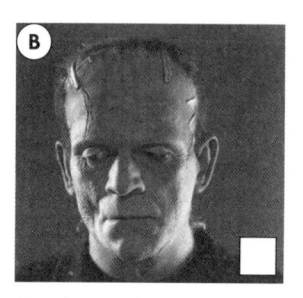

B
Frankenstein: Frankenstein's Monster

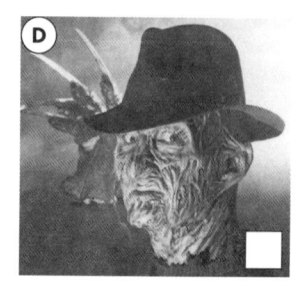

C
Dracula

D
Nightmare on Elm Street: Freddie

b ▶ CD2 T20 Listen again and complete the sentences.

1. People have always been fascinated by monsters and the dark side ....
2. Without evil there is no such thing ....
3. The late .... and early part of the .... was the golden age of the monster.
4. Frankenstein's Monster and Mr Hyde were the results of humans trying to ....
5. .... have no motivation. They're very two-dimensional.
6. Freddie, Jason and Michael Myers are really just three ....
7. Audiences just want to see how many ....
8. All these monsters do is make us scared to go to ....

LISTENING TIP

How to complete sentences

- As with all listening exercises, read through the questions carefully before you listen. This will help prepare you for what you might expect to hear.
- Try to predict what the missing word(s) might be. However, remember that your predictions may be wrong, so you still need to listen carefully to check.
- You will not always hear the exact words that are in the question. Listen carefully for different words that are used that have the same meaning.

  For example, question 1 says:

  <u>People</u> have always been <u>fascinated by</u> monsters.

  You heard:

  <u>The human race</u> has always been <u>extremely interested in</u> monsters.

- You are only expected to write between one and three words. No more.
- Finally, read through your answers carefully. Make sure they are grammatically correct and check your spelling.

Unit check

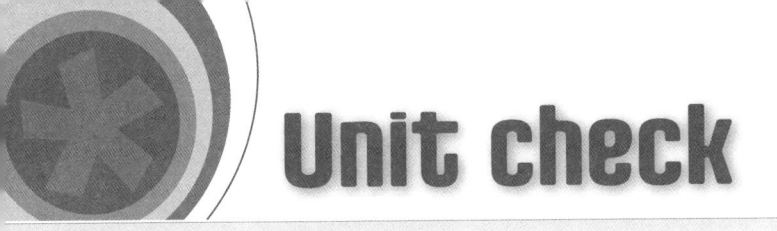

1 Fill in the spaces

Complete the text with the words in the box.

> getting to get to play imagination
> characters strategy ~~entertainment~~
> graphics playing popularity

The best form of _entertainment_ for me is a good computer game. One with cool ¹_____ that seem like real people. And it has to have good ²_____, so that you feel like you're right there in the action. I don't like games that are too simple. I like trying to work out the ³_____ of the game – you know, I enjoy ⁴_____ into the mind of the game's creator. The best games need a lot of ⁵_____, because there are so many boring games out there. The ⁶_____ of a game doesn't really matter to me – just because everyone wants ⁷_____ it doesn't mean it's good. I actually don't mind ⁸_____ older games. I'd love ⁹_____ the original PacMan one day – it's amazing.

[ ] 9

2 Choose the correct answers

Circle the correct answer: a, b or c.

1 Stephen Spielberg's got such a fantastic _____.
  a imagine b imaginity c (imagination)

2 I must remember _____ the DVD back to the shop today.
  a taking b to take c take

3 I like a computer game that _____ me, and makes me think.
  a challenges b strategies c controls

4 That teacher is well known for her _____.
  a kind b kindly c kindness

5 You should _____ drinking too many fizzy drinks. They're not good for you.
  a choose b avoid c afford

6 They don't feel like _____ to the party tonight.
  a going b to going c to go

7 My parents don't _____ about anything.
  a agree b agreement c agreeing

8 After walking six kilometres, they stopped _____ a drink and a rest.
  a to have b having c have

9 I suggested _____ a cheaper phone, but he didn't listen.
  a buy b you to buy c buying

[ ] 8

3 Vocabulary

Complete the sentences with nouns made from the underlined words.

1 He thinks it's possible, but I don't see any _possibility_ of it happening.

2 Are they different? I can't see any _____ between them.

3 So what if he's popular! I don't care about _____.

4 Did you say you want me to protect you? Why do you need _____?

5 You're so creative! I wish I had your _____.

6 Please don't punish me. I can't stand _____.

7 A: Did you enjoy the game?
  B: It wasn't what I'd call _____.

8 I've been preparing for this all week. That's enough _____.

9 She reacted badly. In fact, I was really surprised at her _____.

[ ] 8

How did you do?

Total: [ ] 25

| 😊 Very good 20 – 25 | 😐 OK 14 – 19 | ☹ Review Unit 8 again 0 – 13 |

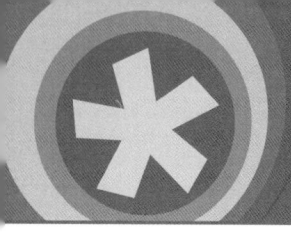

Grammar reference

Unit 2

Past simple vs. present perfect simple

1. We use the past simple to talk about complete events which are finished, or before 'now', the moment of speaking.
   I **called** you yesterday. Where **were** you?
   We **didn't have** computers when I **was** born.

2. We use the present perfect simple to connect the past and 'now', the moment of speaking.
   We**'ve called** you three times today. Where **have** you **been**?
   We**'ve lived** in the same house all our lives.

3. Use the past simple with *minutes ago, yesterday, last week, when I was …* etc.
   We often use *for, since, just, already, yet, ever* and *never* with the present perfect.
   They **went** out a few minutes **ago**.   They**'ve just left**.
   I **saw** that film **yesterday**.   I**'ve already seen** that film.
   I **met** her boyfriend **last weekend**.   I**'ve never met** your girlfriend.
   We **moved** there **when I was young**.   We**'ve lived** there **since I was a child**.

Time expressions

1. We use *just* before the past participle to say that something happened a short time ago.
   We**'ve just arrived**.   They**'ve just gone** out.

2. We use *already* at the end of the sentence or before the past participle to express surprise or emphasise that something happened.
   Have you **finished already**?   We**'ve already seen** this film.

3. We use *yet* at the end of negative sentences to emphasise that something didn't happen (but probably will in the future), and at the end of questions.
   I **haven't started** this exercise **yet**. (but I will)   Have you **met** my new boyfriend **yet**?

4. We use *still* before *haven't* in negative sentences, or before *not* in questions, to show surprise that something you expected to happen didn't happen.
   I can't believe you **still haven't said** sorry.   Has she **still not told** you the truth?

Unit 3

Past simple vs. past continuous

1. We use the past simple to talk about actions that happened at one moment in time in the past. We use the past continuous to describe the background actions in progress around that time in the past.
   I **was playing** football. (background)   I **broke** my leg. (action)
   We **were having** a picnic. (background)   It **started** to rain. (action)
   What **were** you **doing**? (background)   I **called** you. (action)

2. It is common to use *when* with the past simple to introduce the past action, or *while* with the past continuous to introduce the background.
   I **broke** my leg **while** I **was playing** football.
   We **were having** a picnic **when** it **started** to rain.
   What **were** you **doing when** I **called** you?

Time conjunctions: *as / then / as soon as*

Other time words that we use with the past simple are *then* and *as soon as*. We can also use *as* with the same meaning as *while*.
As soon as I **got** home, I turned on the TV for the big game.
The picture came on, **then** I **learned** the bad news.
Someone scored **as** I **was making** a sandwich.

GRAMMAR REFERENCE

Past simple vs. past perfect

1. We use the past simple to talk about an event that happened at a specific time in the past.
   We use the past perfect when we need to emphasise that one event happened <u>before</u> another.
   The match **had started** when we **got** there.
   When I **got** to the street I **realised** I **hadn't brought** his address with me.
   How long **had** you **been** there when they finally **arrived**?

2. Sometimes it is necessary to use the past perfect to make the meaning clear.
   She'**d left** when I got there. (I didn't see her.)
   She **left** when I got there. (but I saw her.)

3. It is not necessary to use the past perfect when *before* or *after* is used.
   She left **before** I got there.

Unit 4

Present perfect simple vs. present perfect continuous

1. We use the present perfect simple to emphasise the result or completion of an activity.
   I'**ve copied** that CD you asked me for. Here it is.
   I'**ve bought** everybody's presents. Aren't I organised!

   We use the present perfect continuous to emphasise the activity, not the result or completion of the activity (it may not be finished).
   I'**ve been copying** CD's all morning. Great fun!
   I'**ve been shopping** for presents. That's why I wasn't here.

2. We use the present perfect simple to emphasise 'how many'.
   I'**ve done** ten exercises this morning.
   How many sandwiches **have** you **made**?
   You'**ve had** three pieces of cake already!

   We use the present perfect continuous to emphasise 'how long'.
   I'**ve been doing** exercises for hours.
   How long **have** you **been making** sandwiches?
   You'**ve been eating** cake since you got here!

had better / should / ought to

We use *should* or *ought to* to give advice, or say what we think is a good (or bad) idea. They have the same meaning. Remember, *should* is a modal verb, and is used without *to*. We use *had better* to give stronger advice or warnings. The form is always past (never *have better*), but the meaning is present. *Had better* is also used without *to*.

You **should** take a rest.
She **ought to** be more careful.
He'**d better** start doing some work.

You **shouldn't** worry so much.
She **ought not to** be so pessimistic.
He'**d better not** come near me.

Unit 5

Future predictions

100% probability	will	
↑	will probably	is likely
	might / might not	
↓	probably won't	isn't likely to
0% probability	won't	

When we make predictions about the future, we can use *will*, *might* and *be likely to* (and their negative forms) to show how sure we are about the chances of something happening.
My parents **will be** really angry when I get home tonight. (100% sure)
My father **will probably** / **is likely to shout** at me.
They **might not let** me **go out** again next weekend.
My brother **probably won't** / **isn't likely to help** me.
But next weekend, my parents **won't remember** what happened!

First conditional with *if* and *unless*

In first conditional sentences:
a both verbs refer to actions or events in the future;
b the verb tense after the words *if* or *unless* is present simple;
c the verb tense in the other clause is *will* or *won't*;
d we can use *if* or *unless* (which means 'if not');
e when we use *unless*, the verb that follows is in the positive.

*If my friends **visit** me (tomorrow), we'**ll go** out for lunch.*
*I'**ll take** them to the Chinese restaurant, unless they **want** to eat pizza. (= .... if they **don't want** to eat pizza.)*
*Unless my parents give me some money, I **won't be able** to pay. (= If my parents **don't give** ...)*

Unit 6

make / let / be allowed to

1 We use *make* [*someone do*] to talk about an obligation.
   *Our teacher **makes us do** a lot of homework. (= We cannot choose, it's an obligation that our teacher gives us.)*
   *My older brother **made me lend** him some money. (= I could not choose, my brother forced me.)*

2 We use *let* [*someone do*] to talk about permission.
   *Our teacher **lets us leave** early on Fridays. (= The teacher gives us permission to leave early.)*
   *My father **let me use** the car yesterday. (= My father gave me permission to use the car.)*

3 We use *be allowed to* [*do something*] to say that someone has (or has not) got permission.
   *At our school, we'**re allowed to wear** jeans if we want to.*
   *When we were young, we **weren't allowed to play** outside in the street.*

Modals of obligation, prohibition and permission

1 *have to / don't have to* is used to talk about obligation / no obligation.
   *We **don't have to wear** school uniform. (= Wearing school uniform is not an obligation for us.)*
   *We **didn't have to pay** for the meal. (= It was not necessary to pay.)*

2 *can / can't* is used to talk about permission.
   *You **can watch** TV if you want to. (= I give you permission to watch TV.)*
   *We **can't go** in because we're not 18. (= We don't have permission to go in.)*

3 We use *mustn't* to prohibit someone from doing something, or to say that something is very important.
   *We **mustn't be** late! (= It is very important for us not to be late.)*
   *You **mustn't talk** to me like that! (= I am telling you that I don't allow this.)*

Unit 7

Present and past passive review

We form the passive with a form of the verb *to be* + the past participle of the main verb.
*English **is spoken** all over the world.*   *My bike **was stolen** last night.*

Present perfect passive

We form the present perfect passive with *have/has been* + past participle.
*Our old house isn't there any more – it'**s been pulled** down.*
*The rules of tennis **haven't been changed** for a long time.*

Future passive

We form the future passive with *will be / won't be* + past participle.
*Those trees **will be cut** down next month.*
*If you don't behave properly, you **won't be invited** again!*

Causative *have* (*have something done*)

We use *have something done* when we talk about a service or function that someone else does for us.
*I **had my hair cut** last week. (= I went to a hairdresser and a person cut my hair.)*
*We'**ve had our car repaired**. (= We've taken our car to a garage and someone has repaired it for us.)*

Unit 8

Gerunds and infinitives

1 When a verb is followed by another verb, the second verb is either in the gerund (-ing) or infinitive form. The form of the second verb depends on the first verb.

2 Some verbs (e.g. *enjoy, detest, (don't) mind, imagine, feel like, suggest, practise, miss*) are followed by a verb in the gerund form.
   *I don't **enjoy living** in the city very much.*   *She doesn't **feel like going** out tonight.*

3 Other verbs (e.g. *hope, promise, ask, learn, expect, decide, afford, offer, choose*) are followed by a verb in the infinitive form.
   *We can't **afford to go** on holiday this year.*   *I **promise to pay** you on Monday.*

Verbs with gerunds or infinitives

1 Some verbs (e.g. *remember, stop, try*) can be followed by a second verb in either the gerund or infinitive form. The form of the second verb depends on the meaning of the sentence.
   *I **remember going** to my first football match with my dad. (= I remember the occasion.)*
   *I **remembered to go** to the stadium and buy the tickets. (= I promised my son I would buy the tickets and I didn't forget to do this.)*
   *I **stopped to watch** the news headlines. (= I was doing something (my homework / talking to my parents) when the news started. I stopped the first activity because I wanted to watch the headlines.)*
   *I **stopped watching** TV and went to bed. (= I was watching TV. I was tired so I turned off the TV and went to bed.)*

2 Some verbs (e.g. *like, love, hate, prefer, begin, start*) can be followed by gerund or infinitive with no difference in meaning.
   *We **began to run** when it **started raining**.*   *We **began running** when it **started to rain**.*

4 Sometimes the information is additional. We don't need it to understand what we are talking about. This is a non-defining relative clause. The extra information is included between commas. (NB In these sentences we <u>can't</u> use *that*.) For example:
   *My brother, **who lives in Canada**, is an architect.*
   (= I only have one brother. He lives in Canada and is an architect.)

Acknowledgements

The publishers are grateful to the following for permission to reproduce photographic material:

Key: l = left, c = centre, r = right, t = top, b = bottom

Alamy/©GFC Collection p 83 (l); ©BBC/Adam Pensotti p 108 (b); Getty Images/The Bridgeman Art Library/Nigerian p 83 (r), /Iconica/Jamie Grill p 94 (4), /The Image Bank/DreamPictures p 94 (8), /Taxi/Biddiboo p 94 (7), /Taxi/Judith Haeusler p 76; The Kobal Collection/DANJAQ/EON/UA/Keith Hamshere p 117, /New Line p 120 (D), /Paramount p 120 (A), /Universal p 120 (B, C); Photolibrary.com/Cultura/Bill Holden p 94 (1), /Kablonk p 94 (2), /Pixland p 94 (3), /Stockbroker/Monkey Business Images Ltd p 94 (5), /White p 94 (6); Rex Features p 93, /L.J. van Houten p 107, Barbara Lindberg p 108 (t); Shutterstock Images/Diego Cervo p 114, /Alexia Kruscheva p 81, /privilege p 84.

The publishers are grateful to the following illustrators:

Anna Lazareva c/o Lemonade, David Haughey c/o 3 In A Box, Graham Kennedy, Mark Reihill c/o Lemonade, Mark Watkinson c/o Illustration, Rob McClurken, Rosa Dodd c/o NB Illustration, Tracey Knight c/o Lemonade

The publishers are grateful to the following contributors:

Hilary Fletcher: picture research
Eoin Higgins: editorial work
Anne Rosenfeld/Dave Morritt: Workbook audio recordings
Pentacor plc: design and layouts

DVD-ROM Instructions

START THE DVD-ROM

Windows PC
- Insert the *English in Mind* DVD-ROM into your DVD-ROM drive.
- If Autorun is enabled, the DVD-ROM will start automatically.
- If Autorun is not enabled, open **My Computer** and then **D:** (where D is the letter of your DVD-ROM drive). Then double-click on the *Run English in Mind 3 from the DVD* icon.

Mac OS X
- Insert the *English in Mind* DVD-ROM into your DVD-ROM drive.
- Double-click on the DVD-ROM icon on your desktop to open it.
- Double-click on the *English in Mind 3 Mac OS X* icon.

INSTALL THE DVD-ROM TO YOUR HARD DISK (RECOMMENDED)

Windows PC
- Go to **My Computer** and then **D:** (where D is the letter of your DVD-ROM drive).
- Right-click and select *Explore*.
- Double-click on *setup*.
- Follow the installation instructions on your screen.

Mac OS X
- Double-click on the DVD-ROM icon on your desktop to open it.
- Create a folder on your computer.
- Copy the content of the DVD-ROM into this folder.
- Double-click on the *English in Mind 3 Mac OS X* icon.

WHAT'S ON THE DVD-ROM?

- **Workbook audio**
  Your DVD-ROM contains all the audio files that accompany the *English in Mind* Workbook. To access these files double click on the *Run English in Mind 3 from the DVD* icon. On the menu screen that then appears, select *Workbook Audio*.

- **Interactive practise activities**
  Practise your grammar, vocabulary, pronunciation, writing, speaking and listening skills. Click on one of the unit pairs at the top of the screen. Choose an exercise from the skills menu and click on it to start. Click on the *Progress* tab on the left of the screen to see the exercises you have completed and your score.

- **Games**
  Click on the *Games* icon in the top-right of the screen to test your English skills and play the exciting 'World on Wheels' game.

- **Wordlist**
  Click on the *Wordlist* tab on the left of the screen to review vocabulary, see word definitions and listen to correct pronunciations.

- **Tests**
  Create your own tests to practise your grammar and vocabulary. Click on the *Test* tab on the left of the screen, select the units and number of questions you would like for your test and then click Start.

SYSTEM REQUIREMENTS

- 512MB of RAM (1GB recommended for video)
- 1.4GB free hard disk space (if installing to hard disk)
- 800 x 600 resolution or higher
- speakers or headphones
- a microphone if you wish to record yourself speaking

For PC
- Windows® XP, Vista or 7

For Mac
- Mac OSX® 10.4, 10.5 or 10.6
- 1.2 GHz G4 processor or higher

SUPPORT

If you experience difficulties with this DVD-ROM, please visit: www.cambridge.org/elt/multimedia/help

ONLINE GAMES

Register on our website for access to more free games and activities: www.cambridge.org/elt/englishinmind